2018 SQA Specimen and Past Papers with Answers

National 5
GRAPHIC COMMUNICATION

2017 & 2018 Exams
and 2017 Specimen Question Paper

Hodder Gibson Study Skills Advice – National 5 Graphic Communication	– page 3
Hodder Gibson Study Skills Advice – General	– page 5
2017 EXAM	– page 7
2017 SPECIMEN QUESTION PAPER	– page 41
2018 EXAM	– page 75
ANSWERS	– page 111

HODDER
GIBSON
AN HACHETTE UK COMPANY

This book contains the official SQA 2017 and 2018 Exams, and the 2017 Specimen Question Paper for National 5 Graphic Communication, with associated SQA-approved answers modified from the official marking instructions that accompany the paper.

In addition the book contains study skills advice. This advice has been specially commissioned by Hodder Gibson, and has been written by experienced senior teachers and examiners in line with the new National 5 syllabus and assessment outlines. This is not SQA material but has been devised to provide further guidance for National 5 examinations.

Hodder Gibson is grateful to the copyright holders, as credited on the final page of the Answer section, for permission to use their material. Every effort has been made to trace the copyright holders and to obtain their permission for the use of copyright material. Hodder Gibson will be happy to receive information allowing us to rectify any error or omission in future editions.

Hachette UK's policy is to use papers that are natural, renewable and recyclable products and made from wood grown in sustainable forests. The logging and manufacturing processes are expected to conform to the environmental regulations of the country of origin.

Orders: please contact Bookpoint Ltd, 130 Park Drive, Milton Park, Abingdon, Oxon OX14 4SE. Telephone: (44) 01235 827827. Fax: (44) 01235 400454. Lines are open 9.00–5.00, Monday to Saturday, with a 24-hour message answering service. Visit our website at www.hoddereducation.co.uk. Hodder Gibson can also be contacted directly at hoddergibson@hodder.co.uk

This collection first published in 2018 by
Hodder Gibson, an imprint of Hodder Education,
An Hachette UK Company
211 St Vincent Street
Glasgow G2 5QY

Typeset by Aptara, Inc.

Printed in the Spain

A catalogue record for this title is available from the British Library

ISBN: 978-1-5104-5553-5

2 1

2019 2018

Introduction

National 5 Graphic Communication

This book of SQA past papers contains the question papers used in the 2017 and 2018 exams (with answers at the back of the book). A specimen question paper reflecting the content and duration of the exam in 2018 is also included. All of the question papers included in the book provide excellent representative practice for the final exams.

Using these papers as part of your revision will help you to develop the vital skills and techniques needed for the exam, and will help you to identify any knowledge gaps you may have.

It is always a very good idea to refer to SQA's website for the most up-to-date course specification documents. These are available at www.sqa.org.uk/sqa/47459

The course

The aims of the course are to enable you to understand how graphic communication is used every day in design, industry and society and to ensure you learn skills and techniques to create graphics to suit any number of purposes.

The types of graphics you will be able to create include:

- **preliminary** design graphics
- technical **production** drawings
- high-impact **promotional** and information graphics.

These are known as the **3 Ps**.

All of your coursework projects and exam questions are based on these types of graphics. The knowledge you need for the exam will come from the work you do during your project work in class.

How you are assessed and graded

The grade you achieve at the end of the National 5 Graphic Communication course depends on two assessments.

- **Assignment:** this is submitted to SQA before your exam and is worth 40 marks.
- **Question paper:** this is the exam you will sit at the end of the course. It is worth 80 marks.

Your marks for the two assessments are added together to give you a total out of 120 marks.

The exam

Duration: 2 hours

Marks available: 80

The exam will include a mix of short and more extended response questions about the graphics required to design, produce or promote a product.

You should look at the marks awarded for each question. This is a good indicator of the length of answer you should give. For example, for a 3-mark question you will need to make three distinct points, while for a 1-mark question you will need to make only a single point. You should allow yourself around one and a half minutes per mark.

Sketching

Exam questions will be set so that you can answer in writing. Some questions will invite you to use annotated sketches or drawings to support your answer, and space will be provided in the exam booklet for you to sketch these. **Always take this opportunity.**

Remember:

- This is an exam that tests your knowledge and understanding of graphics and you should have all the graphic skills you need.
- It can be easier and quicker to describe your answer graphically with annotations than it is to write about it.
- The quality of sketching will not be assessed but the clarity of your answer is important. So make sure your sketches and annotations are clear.

Skills and knowledge

The exam will test you on the following skills and knowledge:

- **Computer-aided design techniques:** How would you apply 2D and/or 3D CAD techniques to produce a required solution?
- **Creative use of layout, colour and presentation techniques:** How has the graphic designer used design elements and principles and DTP techniques to achieve an effective layout?

- **Manual and electronic methods of graphic communication:** What are the advantages and disadvantages of creating graphics using different methods?
- **Knowledge of drawing standards:** What drawing standards should be applied to orthographic and pictorial drawings?
- **Spatial awareness:** Can you interpret and understand drawings?
- **Graphic items in specific situations:** Why have graphics been used for certain purposes and what impact can graphic items have on society?
- **Graphics and the environment:** How can we create and use graphics without damaging our fragile environment?

Using this book

Practising the type of questions you are likely to face in the National 5 exam is vital if you are to achieve your highest possible grade. This book will give you experience of the problem solving and creative layout questions you will encounter in the exam.

Answering 2D and 3D CAD problem solving questions

You should always:

- study the provided drawing or model
- identify what modelling or drawing techniques have been used
- describe the steps: new sketch, draw profile, select axis, revolve, line, rectangle, circle, etc.
- include the dimensions required
- describe any additional edits used: array, subtract, shell, trim, rotate, etc.
- and, importantly, make annotated sketches to show the steps clearly.

Answering creative layout questions

These questions will ask you to identify how DTP features have been used in a layout and how design elements and principles have been used. Some questions will test your knowledge further by asking you to explain how the use of these features improves the layout.

You should always:

- study the layout (don't rush this!)
- identify the DTP feature(s) and design elements and principles used.
  - Think carefully about how they improve the layout: do they add contrast, create harmony, suggest depth, develop a dominant focal point, unify the layout? The feature you are asked about will do one of these things. Your task is to identify what it does and explain how it does it.

At the end of the exam, don't forget to read over your answers. Read the questions again and double-check that you have answered the question that was asked. You should have plenty of time.

Good luck!

Remember that the rewards for passing National 5 Graphic Communication are well worth it! Your pass will help you get the future you want for yourself. In the exam, be confident in your own ability. If you're not sure how to answer a question, trust your instincts and just give it a go anyway. Keep calm and don't panic! GOOD LUCK!

Oh, and there is a really exciting Higher course waiting for you next year; we'll see you there!

Study Skills – what you need to know to pass exams!

General exam revision: 20 top tips

When preparing for exams, it is easy to feel unsure of where to start or how to revise. This guide to general exam revision provides a good starting place, and, as these are very general tips, they can be applied to all your exams.

1. Start revising in good time.

Don't leave revision until the last minute – this will make you panic and it will be difficult to learn. Make a revision timetable that counts down the weeks to go.

2. Work to a study plan.

Set up sessions of work spread through the weeks ahead. Make sure each session has a focus and a clear purpose. What will you study, when and why? Be realistic about what you can achieve in each session, and don't be afraid to adjust your plans as needed.

3. Make sure you know exactly when your exams are.

Get your exam dates from the SQA website and use the timetable builder tool to create your own exam schedule. You will also get a personalised timetable from your school, but this might not be until close to the exam period.

4. Make sure that you know the topics that make up each course.

Studying is easier if material is in manageable chunks – why not use the SQA topic headings or create your own from your class notes? Ask your teacher for help on this if you are not sure.

5. Break the chunks up into even smaller bits.

The small chunks should be easier to cope with. Remember that they fit together to make larger ideas. Even the process of chunking down will help!

6. Ask yourself these key questions for each course:

- Are all topics compulsory or are there choices?
- Which topics seem to come up time and time again?
- Which topics are your strongest and which are your weakest?

Use your answers to these questions to work out how much time you will need to spend revising each topic.

7. Make sure you know what to expect in the exam.

The subject-specific introduction to this book will help with this. Make sure you can answer these questions:

- How is the paper structured?
- How much time is there for each part of the exam?
- What types of question are involved? These will vary depending on the subject so read the subject-specific section carefully.

8. Past papers are a vital revision tool!

Use past papers to support your revision wherever possible. This book contains the answers and mark schemes too – refer to these carefully when checking your work. Using the mark scheme is useful; even if you don't manage to get all the marks available first time when you first practise, it helps you identify how to extend and develop your answers to get more marks next time – and of course, in the real exam.

9. Use study methods that work well for you.

People study and learn in different ways. Reading and looking at diagrams suits some students. Others prefer to listen and hear material – what about reading out loud or getting a friend or family member to do this for you? You could also record and play back material.

10. There are three tried and tested ways to make material stick in your long-term memory:

- Practising – e.g. rehearsal, repeating
- Organising – e.g. making drawings, lists, diagrams, tables, memory aids
- Elaborating – e.g. incorporating the material into a story or an imagined journey

11. Learn actively.

Most people prefer to learn actively – for example, making notes, highlighting, redrawing and redrafting, making up memory aids, or writing past paper answers. A good way to stay engaged and inspired is to mix and match these methods – find the combination that best suits you. This is likely to vary depending on the topic or subject.

12. Be an expert.

Be sure to have a few areas in which you feel you are an expert. This often works because at least some of them will come up, which can boost confidence.

13. Try some visual methods.

Use symbols, diagrams, charts, flashcards, post-it notes etc. Don't forget – the brain takes in chunked images more easily than loads of text.

14. Remember – practice makes perfect.

Work on difficult areas again and again. Look and read – then test yourself. You cannot do this too much.

15. Try past papers against the clock.

Practise writing answers in a set time. This is a good habit from the start but is especially important when you get closer to exam time.

16. Collaborate with friends.

Test each other and talk about the material – this can really help. Two brains are better than one! It is amazing how talking about a problem can help you solve it.

17. Know your weaknesses.

Ask your teacher for help to identify what you don't know. Try to do this as early as possible. If you are having trouble, it is probably with a difficult topic, so your teacher will already be aware of this – most students will find it tough.

18. Have your materials organised and ready.

Know what is needed for each exam:

- Do you need a calculator or a ruler?
- Should you have pencils as well as pens?
- Will you need water or paper tissues?

19. Make full use of school resources.

Find out what support is on offer:

- Are there study classes available?
- When is the library open?
- When is the best time to ask for extra help?
- Can you borrow textbooks, study guides, past papers, etc.?
- Is school open for Easter revision?

20. Keep fit and healthy!

Try to stick to a routine as much as possible, including with sleep. If you are tired, sluggish or dehydrated, it is difficult to see how concentration is even possible. Combine study with relaxation, drink plenty of water, eat sensibly, and get fresh air and exercise – all these things will help more than you could imagine. Good luck!

NATIONAL 5
2017

N5

National Qualifications 2017

Mark

X735/75/01

Graphic Communication

WEDNESDAY, 10 MAY

1:00 PM – 2:30 PM

Fill in these boxes and read what is printed below.

Full name of centre

Town

Forename(s)

Surname

Number of seat

Date of birth

Day   Month   Year

Scottish candidate number

Total marks — 60

Attempt ALL questions.

All dimensions are in mm.

All technical sketches and drawings use third angle projection.

You may use rulers, compasses or trammels for measuring.

In all questions you may use sketches and annotations to support your answer if you wish.

Write your answers clearly in the spaces provided in this booklet. Additional space for answers is provided at the end of this booklet. If you use this space you must clearly identify the question number you are attempting.

Use **blue** or **black** ink.

Before leaving the examination room you must give this booklet to the Invigilator; if you do not, you may lose all the marks for this paper.

XSQA

[BLANK PAGE]

DO NOT WRITE ON THIS PAGE

Total marks — 60

Attempt ALL questions

1. A company, "Portal", has designed a new range of door handles.

  (a) An exploded isometric line drawing of a door handle was produced for an instruction manual as shown below.

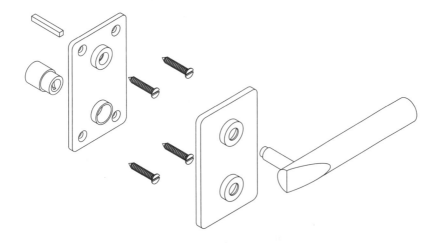

    (i) Describe one benefit of this type of pictorial view.   **1**

_____

_____

    (ii) Describe three areas of good practice that have been applied when producing the exploded view, shown above.   **3**

_____

_____

_____

_____

_____

_____

1. (continued)

Orthographic sectional views, shown below, were produced for manufacture. The fixing screws have been removed for clarity.

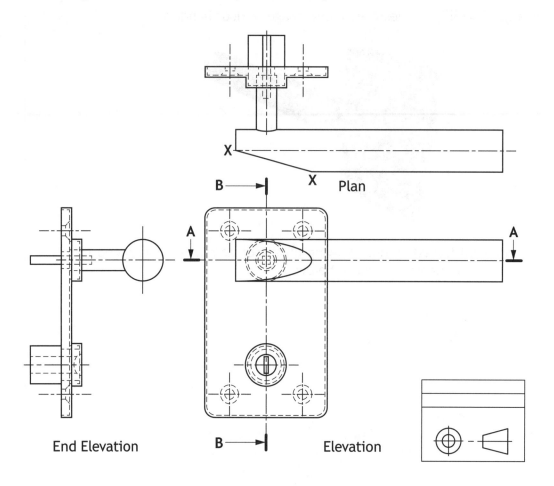

Plan

End Elevation

B

Elevation

(b) Identify the correct sectional plan **A-A** by ticking (✓) a box below.   1

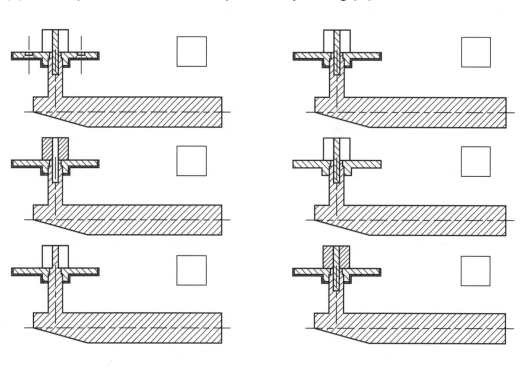

MARKS | DO NOT WRITE IN THIS MARGIN

1. (continued)

(c) Identify the correct sectional end elevation **B-B** by ticking (✓) a box below.   1

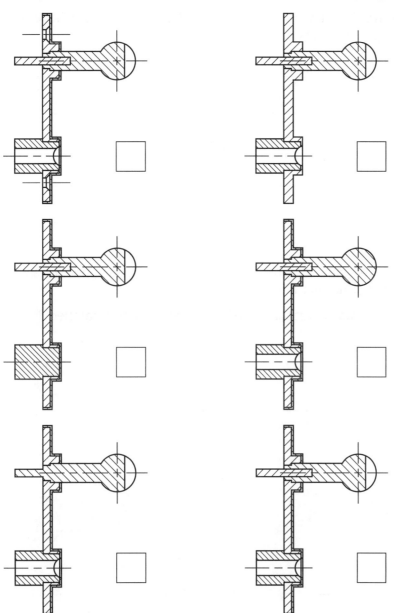

(d) A true shape of cut surface **X-X** was required.

Identify the correct true shape **X-X** by ticking (✓) a box below.   1

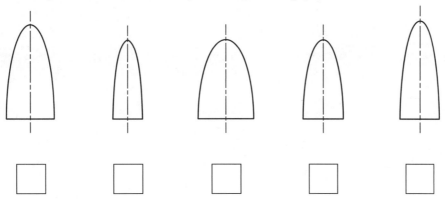

1. (continued)

(e) When producing sectional drawings, different component parts are identified through the use of hatching.

Describe two ways that hatching can be **varied** to aid the identification of different component parts.

2

_____

_____

_____

_____

_____

(f) When producing sectional drawings there are certain components and features that are not normally hatched.

State two components or features that are **not** normally hatched in a sectional view.

2

_____

_____

[Turn over for next question

DO NOT WRITE ON THIS PAGE

1. (continued)

(g) "Portal" want to expand their range of door handles. They have developed an interchangeable design that allows a handle to be removed and replaced.

Assembled CAD illustration

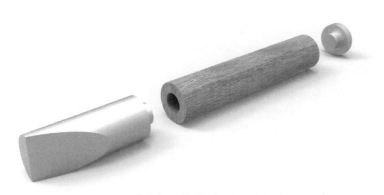

Exploded CAD illustration

An orthographic drawing for one of the handle components is shown below.

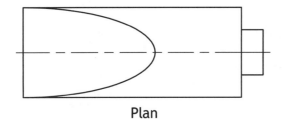

Plan

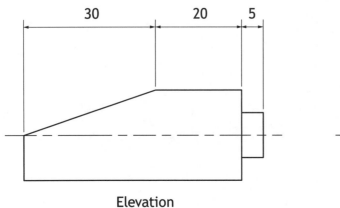

Elevation

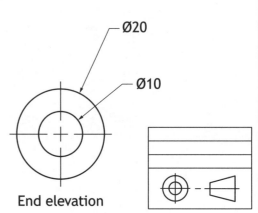

End elevation

Ø20

Ø10

1. (g) (continued)

MARKS

Describe, using the correct dimensions and 3D CAD modelling terms, how you would use 3D CAD software to model the handle component in the orthographic drawing, shown opposite. You may use sketches to support your answer.

4

[Turn over

2. An architectural company have designed a new modular seating system that will be the focal point of a city centre redevelopment. A billboard display will be placed at the site, communicating the design to the public.

Before arriving at the final layout the graphic designer first produced the draft layout, shown below.

Draft layout

The draft layout was then developed. The final layout is shown below.

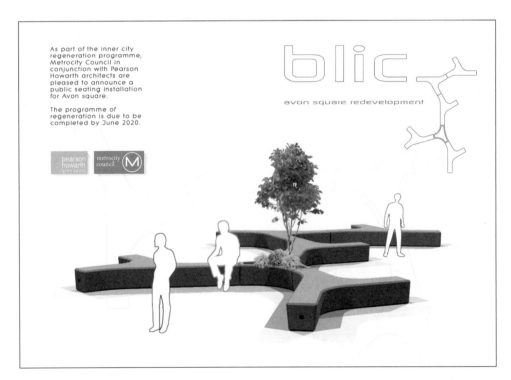

Final layout

2. (continued)

MARKS

(a) Describe how the graphic designer has applied each of the design elements and principles, listed below, to produce the **final layout**.

(i) Alignment   1

_____

_____

_____

_____

(ii) Unity   1

_____

_____

_____

_____

(iii) Contrast   1

_____

_____

_____

_____

[Turn over

2. (continued)

MARKS

(b) The billboard is to be placed on a busy street where pedestrians and traffic will pass by.

Explain how the location of the billboard has influenced the design of the **final layout**.

1

_____

_____

_____

_____

(c) When the graphic designer produced the final layout, the following DTP features were used: **Grid** and **Snap to grid**.

Describe two ways these DTP features assist the graphic designer.

2

_____

_____

_____

_____

_____

_____

_____

2. **(continued)**

(d) The design of the seating system allows a number of different arrangements to be created.

An orthographic assembled plan of one arrangement is shown below.

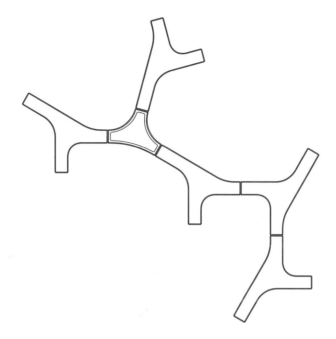

Identify the **two** pictorial assembly drawings that match the arrangement shown above in the orthographic assembled plan, by ticking (✓) two boxes below.

2

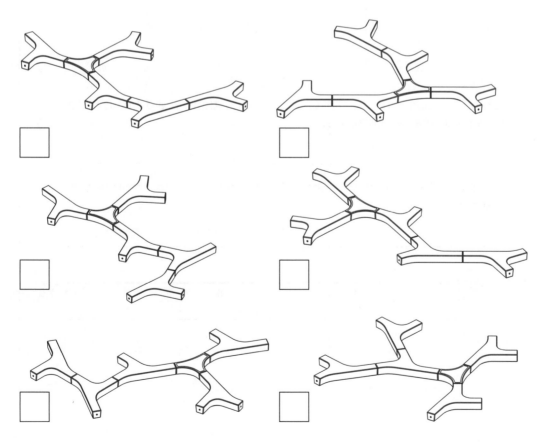

2.   (continued)

The planter component of the seating system was modelled using 3D CAD software. Orthographic drawings of the planter component are shown below.

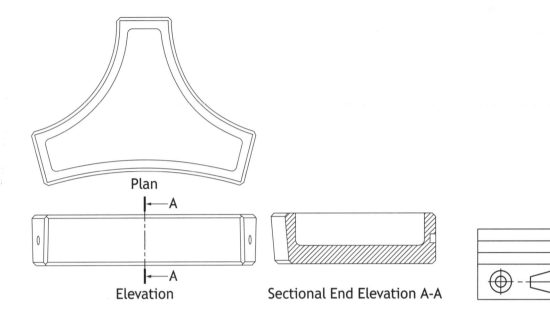

Plan

Elevation   Sectional End Elevation A-A

(e) A CAD technician created a sketch of the planter profile. The first stage of the sketch is shown below.

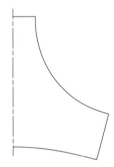

(i)   State the name of the 2D CAD command that would be used to complete the sketch above.

1

_____

(ii) Describe one benefit of using this CAD command in creating this sketch.

1

_____

_____

_____

2. (continued)

(f) From the 2D sketch, Stage 1 was produced. Further stages of the 3D CAD model are shown below.

Stage 1

Stage 2

Stage 3

Stage 4

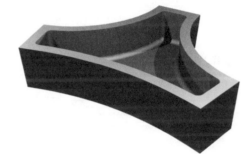
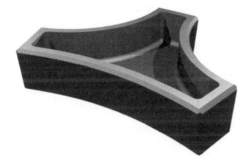

At each stage a 3D CAD modelling **feature or edit** has been used.

State the 3D CAD modelling **feature or edit** used in creating each stage. Stage 1 is already given.

You should refer to the orthographic drawings shown opposite.

Stage 1 _Loft_

(i) Stage 2 _____ 1

(ii) Stage 3 _____ 1

(iii) Stage 4 _____ 1

[Turn over

2. (continued)

MARKS

Illustrated views of two of the seating modules are shown below.

Locating peg   Socket

(g) The components are connected by locating pegs and sockets.

(i) Indicate, by **shading,** the relevant **surfaces** and state, using 3D CAD terms, how you would assemble and constrain the given components.

5

Stage one has been shaded for you.

Stage one

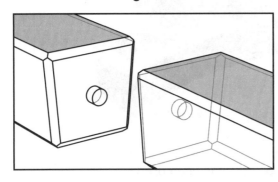

Constraint used

_____

Stage two

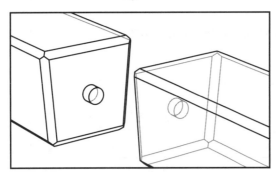

Constraint used

_____

Stage three

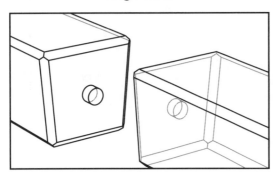

Constraint used

_____

2. (g) (continued)

MARKS

DO NOT WRITE IN THIS MARGIN

The seating system was added to a library of standard components.

(ii) Describe two ways a CAD library can assist the design process.

2

_____

_____

_____

_____

_____

_____

[Turn over

MARKS

3. "Colour Hive" is an educational toy designed to teach children about colour mixing. Each toy is a hexagonal tile that emits a primary colour. The colour is controlled through the use of a smartphone app.

The tiles are designed to be stackable. When a second coloured tile is stacked on top of the first, the colours of each tile are mixed to produce a secondary colour.

(a) Complete the table below to show the top tile and resultant colours.   3

Bottom Tile	Top Tile	Resultant Colour
Red	Yellow	
Yellow		Green
Blue		Violet

3. (continued)

MARKS | DO NOT WRITE IN THIS MARGIN

The smartphone app used to control the tiles is shown below.

(b) The tints and shades of the tiles can also be controlled by using the smartphone app.

State how to create a shade of a colour.   1

_____

_____

(c) Contrasting colours were used in the colour scheme of this smartphone app.

Explain why **contrast** is important in the design of the smartphone app.   1

_____

_____

_____

[Turn over

3. (continued)

MARKS | DO NOT WRITE IN THIS MARGIN

(d) The surface development for the packaging of one "Colour Hive" tile is shown below.

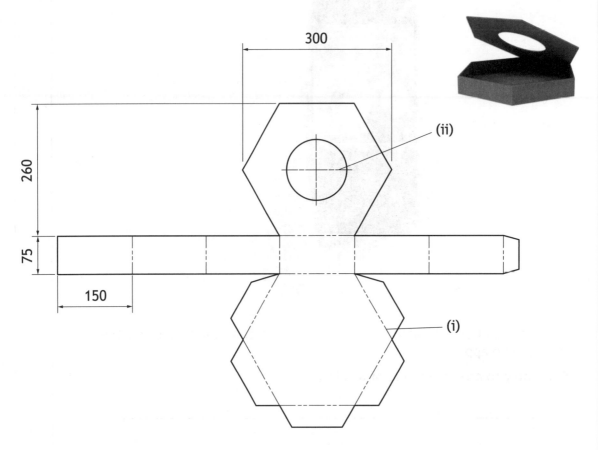

State the line types shown at (i) and (ii).

(i) _____ **1**

(ii) _____ **1**

MARKS | DO NOT WRITE IN THIS MARGIN

4. A company, "Eco Future", has created sets of educational cards that teach children about renewable energy in Scotland. One of the cards is shown below.

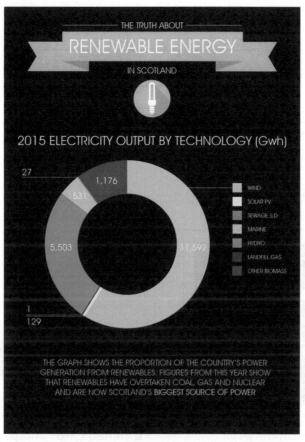

Card 1

(a) State the name of the type of chart used on the card. **1**

_____

(b) Explain, giving two reasons, why this choice of chart is appropriate for communicating this type of information. **2**

_____

_____

_____

_____

[Turn over

4. (continued)

MARKS

The designer used DTP software to produce the graphics on the cards. The same colour scheme was used for all of the cards.

(c) Describe two ways the designer could use the DTP software to ensure the same colour scheme was used on every card.

2

_____

_____

_____

_____

The packaging and printed cards, prior to trimming, are shown below.

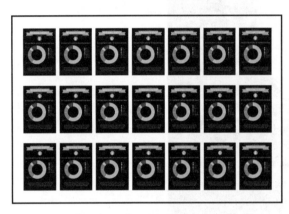

Cards prior to trimming

Trimmed cards and packaging

(d) Describe three ways the cards and packaging could be produced to reduce the impact on the environment.

3

You should refer to both materials **and** printing methods in your answer.

_____

_____

_____

_____

_____

_____

MARKS | DO NOT WRITE IN THIS MARGIN

5. "(S)TABLE" is a flat-pack stool/table designed using 3D CAD modelling software. A promotional graphic that includes a 3D CAD illustration of the product is shown below.

You should refer to the **Supplementary Sheets for use with Question 5** before answering all parts of this question.

(S)TABLE

OAK LEGS THAT SLOT TOGETHER

BEAUTIFUL **MAHOGANY** ROUND SEAT

ONE SINGLE **BEECH** DOWEL

The product is designed to fit together without any gaps in the joints.

(a) State the following missing dimensions on the orthographic drawing shown on **Supplementary Sheet 1 for use with Question 5.**

    (i)   Diameter A: _____   **1**

    (ii) Height B: _____   **1**

    (iii) Length C: _____   **1**

    (iv) Length D: _____   **1**

[Turn over

MARKS | DO NOT WRITE IN THIS MARGIN

5.   (continued)

(b) The dowel is made to the exact dimensions in order to fit tightly into the Seat and Leg 2.

You should refer to the Supplementary Sheets for use with Question 5.

(i) Add the dimensions, correct to British Standard conventions, to the dowel below.

2

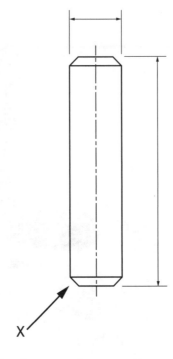

(ii) State the name of the feature shown at X.

1

_____

(c) An elevation of the assembled product with a cutting plane is shown below.

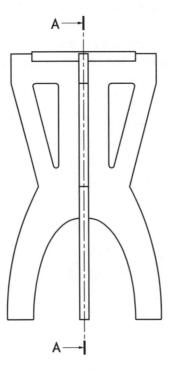

5. (c) (continued)

MARKS | DO NOT WRITE IN THIS MARGIN

Identify the correct sectional end elevation **A-A** by ticking (✓) a box below.　1

You should refer to the elevation shown opposite and the **Supplementary Sheets for use with Question 5.**

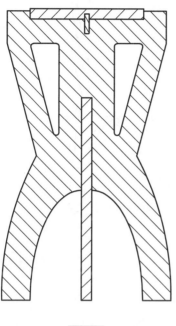

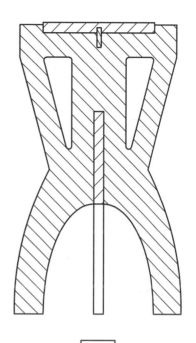

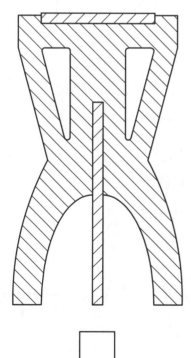

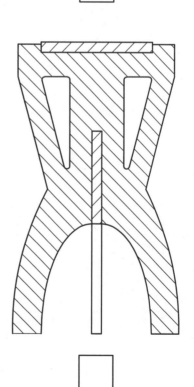

[Turn over

5.   (continued)

(d)   Identify the **two** correct pictorial views of the product by ticking (✓) two boxes below.

2

You should refer to the **Supplementary Sheets for use with Question 5.**

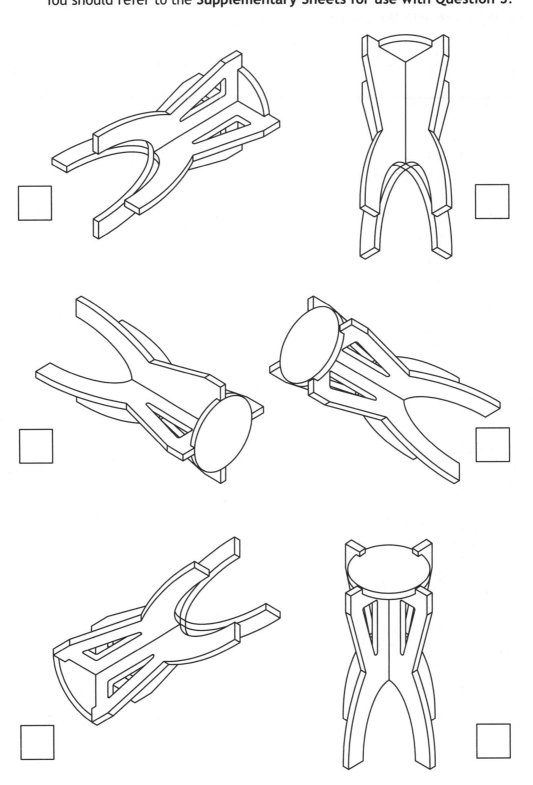

[END OF QUESTION PAPER]

MARKS | DO NOT WRITE IN THIS MARGIN

ADDITIONAL SPACE FOR ANSWERS

MARKS | DO NOT WRITE IN THIS MARGIN

ADDITIONAL SPACE FOR ANSWERS

National Qualifications 2017

X735/75/11

Graphic Communication
Supplementary Sheets

WEDNESDAY, 10 MAY

1:00 PM — 2:30 PM

Supplementary Sheets for use with Question 5.

Supplementary Sheet 1 for use with Question 5

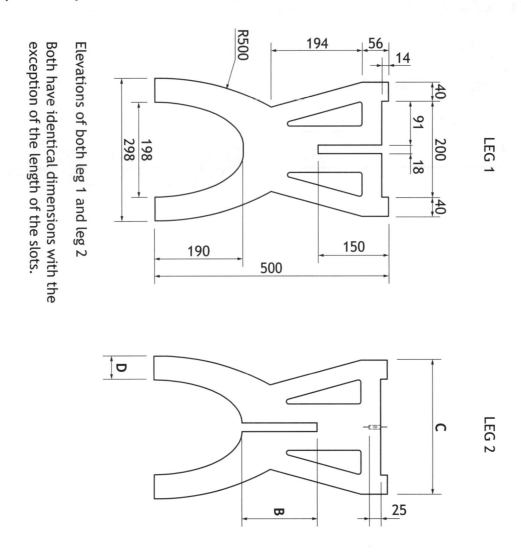

Elevations of both leg 1 and leg 2

Both have identical dimensions with the exception of the length of the slots.

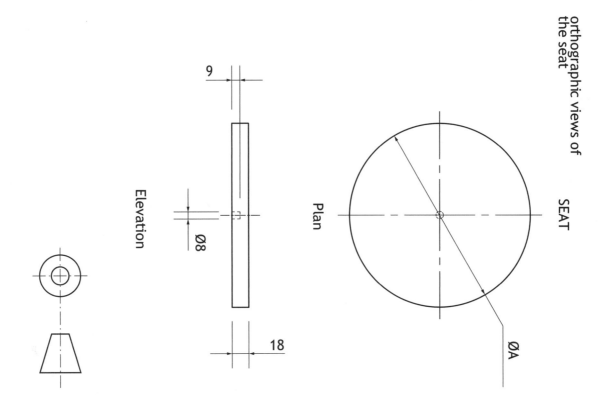

orthographic views of the seat

Supplementary Sheet 2 for use with Question 5

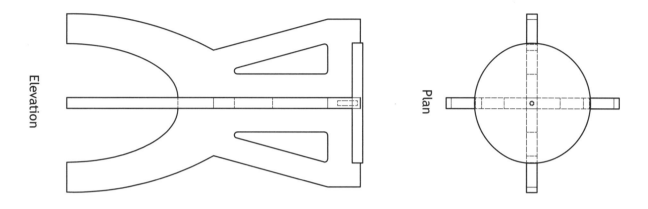

Elevation

Plan

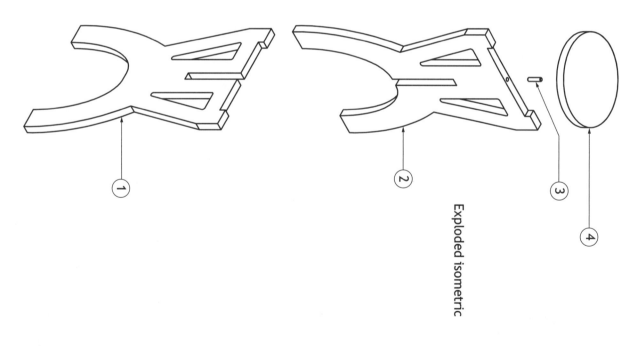

Exploded isometric

[BLANK PAGE]

DO NOT WRITE ON THIS PAGE

NATIONAL 5

2017 Specimen Question Paper

HODDER
GIBSON
LEARN MORE

FOR OFFICIAL USE

N5

National Qualifications
SPECIMEN ONLY

Mark

S835/75/01

Graphic Communication

Date — Not applicable

Duration — 2 hours

Fill in these boxes and read what is printed below.

Full name of centre

Town

Forename(s)

Surname

Number of seat

Date of birth

Day   Month   Year   Scottish candidate number

Total marks — 80

Attempt ALL questions.

All dimensions are in mm.

All technical sketches and drawings use third angle projection.

You may use rulers, compasses or trammels for measuring.

In all questions you may use sketches and annotations to support your answer if you wish.

Write your answers clearly in the spaces provided in this booklet. Additional space for answers is provided at the end of this booklet. If you use this space you must clearly identify the question number you are attempting.

Use **blue** or **black** ink.

Before leaving the examination room you must give this booklet to the Invigilator; if you do not, you may lose all the marks for this paper.

MARKS | DO NOT WRITE IN THIS MARGIN

Total marks — 80

Attempt ALL questions

1. A company is promoting a new wireless speaker using a webpage. A graphic designer has produced a series of thumbnails for the design of the webpage.

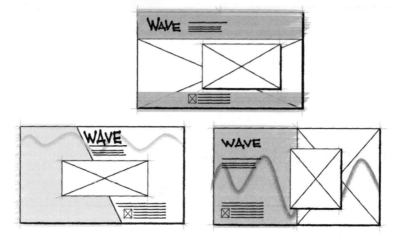

(a) State two reasons why thumbnail sketches would be produced during the preliminary stages.

2

_____

_____

_____

_____

MARKS | DO NOT WRITE IN THIS MARGIN

1.   **(continued)**

The graphic designer selected one of the thumbnails and decided to use DTP software to develop the initial idea. The thumbnail is shown below with the designer's annotations showing suggested changes.

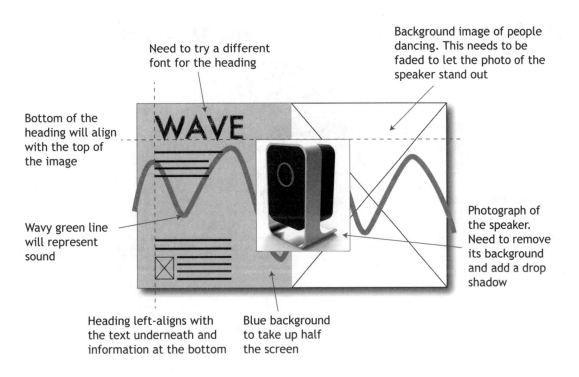

Need to try a different font for the heading

Background image of people dancing. This needs to be faded to let the photo of the speaker stand out

Bottom of the heading will align with the top of the image

Wavy green line will represent sound

Photograph of the speaker. Need to remove its background and add a drop shadow

Heading left-aligns with the text underneath and information at the bottom

Blue background to take up half the screen

The graphic designer used the above thumbnail annotations to develop the design using DTP software.

(b) Explain three advantages to the graphic designer of using DTP software to produce a graphic layout.   3

_____

_____

_____

_____

_____

_____

_____

[Turn over

1.   (continued)

The final design for the webpage is shown below.

(c)   Describe the effect to the webpage of using the **green lines**.   2

_____

_____

_____

_____

(d)   Explain how the graphic designer has used the following design elements and principles to create visual impact in the final design.

    (i)   Depth   2

      _____

      _____

      _____

      _____

MARKS | DO NOT WRITE IN THIS MARGIN

1. (d) (continued)

      (ii) Dominance   2

      (iii) Alignment   2

  (e) Transparency has been applied to the image of the people dancing in the webpage shown opposite.

      Describe why the graphic designer has used the desktop publishing technique "transparency" on this image.   1

  (f) Describe how the desktop publishing technique "bleed" has been used in the webpage design shown opposite.   1

The company originally planned on using posters to promote its product.

  (g) Describe the **positive** impact to the environment of using a webpage rather than printed posters to promote the product.   2

           [Turn over

MARKS | DO NOT WRITE IN THIS MARGIN

2. ECHO is a new fragrance. The bottle and packaging have been designed to reflect the product name.

The centre 'O'ring consists of **two interlocking parts** that secure the bottle in the packaging.

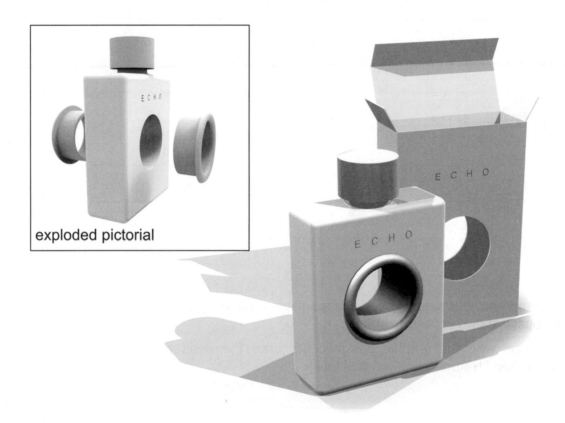

exploded pictorial

The product will be mass produced and sold globally. The company wish to minimise the product's impact on the environment.

(a) Describe two ways the designer can reduce the impact the packaging has on the environment.

2

_____

_____

_____

_____

_____

_____

MARKS | DO NOT WRITE IN THIS MARGIN

2. (continued)

The packaging for the bottle is to be manufactured from a single sheet of card. A surface development of the packaging is shown below.

The CAD technician has been asked to identify the positioning of key features that are to be cut out.

(b) Indicate on the surface development, below, where the text "ECHO" will be cut out.

You should use the CAD illustration provided on the opposite page.

Use "E" to indicate the position of the text.

1

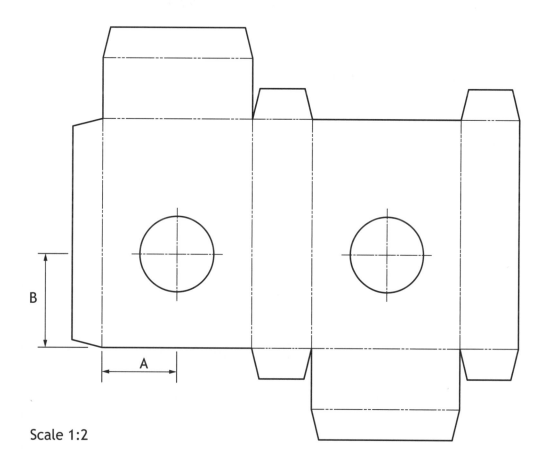

Scale 1:2

(c) Calculate, using the scale 1:2, measurements A and B (indicated on the above development).

Use a ruler to measure.

(i) Measurement A _____ mm

1

(ii) Measurement B _____ mm

1

[Turn over

MARKS | DO NOT WRITE IN THIS MARGIN

2. (continued)

(d) State one factor that would influence the choice of scale in a drawing.   **1**

_____

_____

The CAD technician is unsure which dimensioning technique to use and has applied two different methods shown in the assembled orthographic views provided in the **supplementary sheets for use with question 2(e)**.

(e) (i) State the type of dimensioning used for the elevation.   **1**

_____

(ii) State the type of dimensioning used for the plan.   **1**

_____

2.   **(continued)**

Orthographic sectional views were produced to aid manufacture.

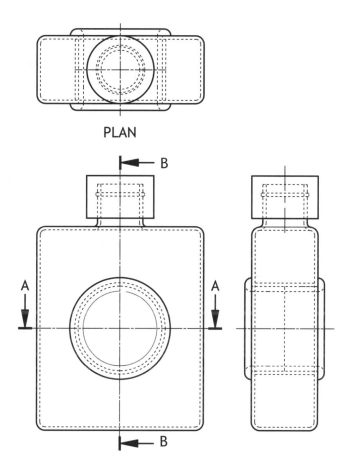

PLAN

(f)   Identify the correct sectional plan **A-A**, indicated in the drawing above, by ticking a box below.

1

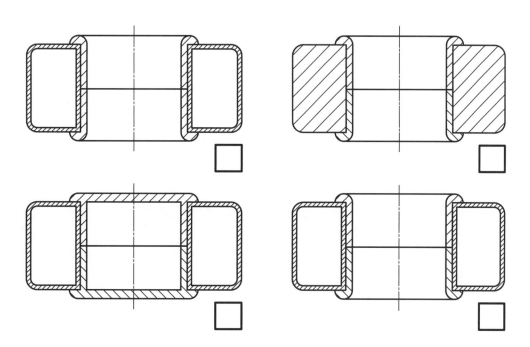

MARKS | DO NOT WRITE IN THIS MARGIN

2.   (continued)

(g)   Identify the correct sectional end elevation **B-B**, indicated in the drawing on the previous page, by ticking a box below.

1

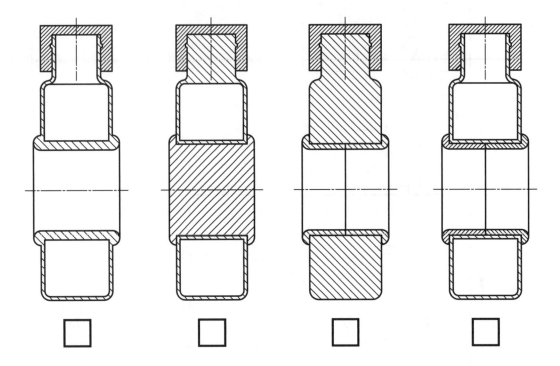

3.   A portable container for storing earphones and other cable accessories is shown below.

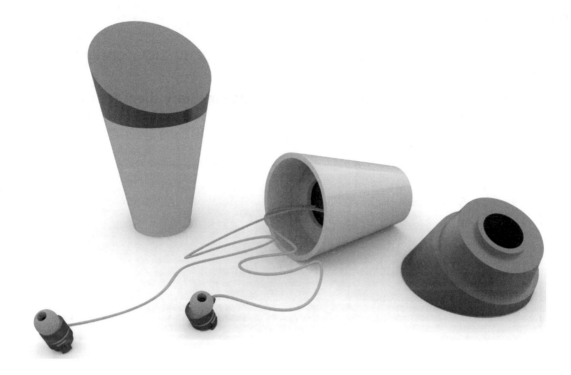

[Turn over

MARKS | DO NOT WRITE IN THIS MARGIN

3.   (continued)

The lid was modelled using 3D CAD modelling software.

(a) Describe, with reference to correct dimensions and 3D CAD modelling techniques, how the lid can be produced.   **6**

You must use the drawing provided in the supplementary sheet for use with question 3(a).

You may use sketches to support your answer.

MARKS | DO NOT WRITE IN THIS MARGIN

3. (continued)

The CAD technician was asked to generate the true shape of the sloping **surface "X-X"** as indicated in the orthographic drawing, shown in the supplementary sheet for use with question 3(b).

(b) Identify the correct true shape of the sloping **surface "X-X"** by ticking a box below.

You must use the drawing provided in the supplementary sheet for use with question 3(b).

You may use a ruler, compass or trammel for measuring.

1

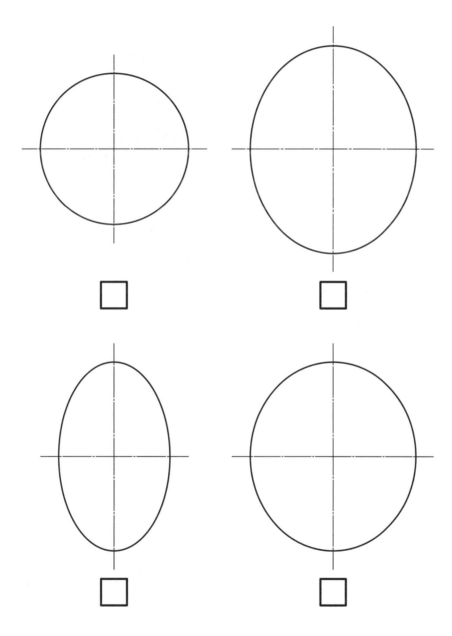

MARKS | DO NOT WRITE IN THIS MARGIN

3.   (continued)

The designer added details to the sloping surface of the lid. The detail consisted of four identical shapes positioned around the centre and raised from the surface.

The initial sketch of one of these shapes is shown in **bold** black. The additional shapes in red were then created using 2D CAD editing commands.

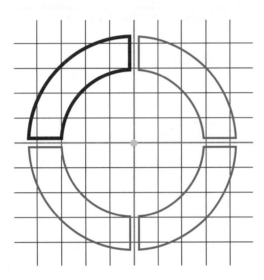   

(c)   Describe, with reference to **2D CAD drawing and editing** commands, how the CAD technician has drawn the initial sketch and then repeated the shape without having to redraw each shape again.

You may use sketches to support your answer.

4

MARKS | DO NOT WRITE IN THIS MARGIN

3.   **(continued)**

The CAD technician extruded the detail on the sloping surface of the lid but also wanted this feature to be shelled along with the other features.

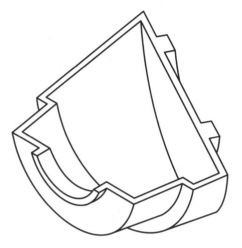

Before

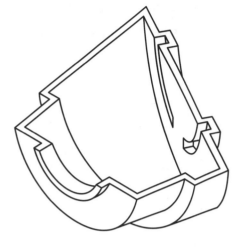

After

(d) Explain how the model could be updated to include the additional shell details.

2

_____

_____

_____

_____

_____

_____

[Turn over

3.   (continued)

The lid and main body of the product were assembled using 3D CAD modelling software.

(e)   Indicate by **shading** the relevant **surfaces** and state using 3D CAD terms how you would insert the lid into the body.

Stage one has been shaded for you.

3

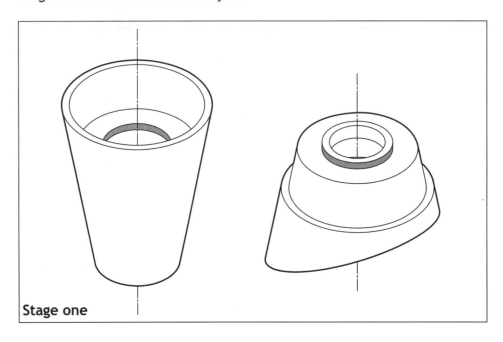

Stage one

Constraint used

_____

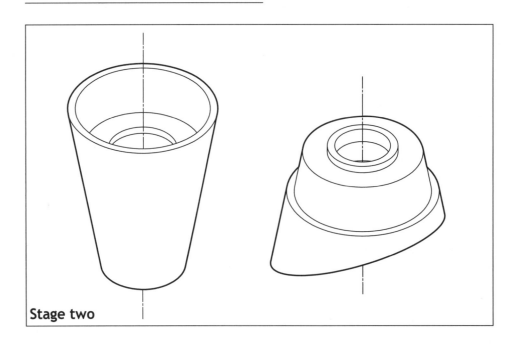

Stage two

Constraint used

_____

MARKS | DO NOT WRITE IN THIS MARGIN

4. A company has designed a range of eco lodges as part of its new holiday park accommodation. The graphic designer produced a flyer detailing the range. The final design is shown below.

Graphics for a construction project fall into 3 main types: *Preliminary, Production* and *Promotional*.

(a) (i) State, from the list given above, the **type** of graphic shown below.   1

_____

(ii) Describe the purpose of this type of graphic.   1

_____

_____

_____

(b) Name the desk top publishing techniques indicated on the final design shown above.

(i) _____   1

(ii) _____   1

(iii) _____   1

(iv) _____   1

(v) _____   1

MARKS | DO NOT WRITE IN THIS MARGIN

4.   **(continued)**

A 3D rendered illustration of the lodge was required for the flyer. The company had this illustration produced by a CAD technician in another country.

(c)   Describe two advantages that **remote working** offers to the company.   2

_____

_____

_____

_____

_____

_____

A plan of the holiday park was drawn up as part of the construction project.

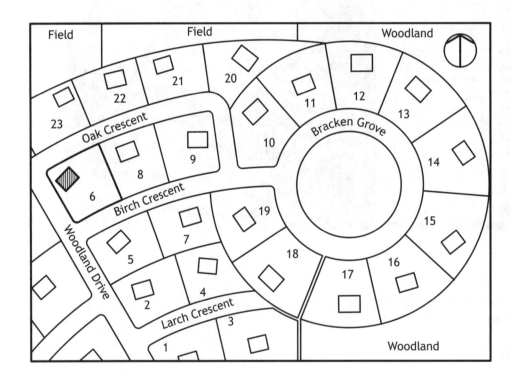

(d)   (i)   State the name of the plan type shown.   1

_____

(ii)   State a scale that is commonly used for this plan type.   1

_____

MARKS | DO NOT WRITE IN THIS MARGIN

4.   **(continued)**

The CAD technician produced pictorial line drawings of the front and rear of the lodge.

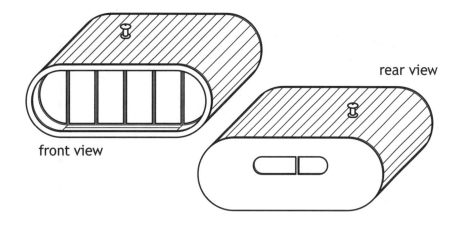

rear view

front view

(e)   (i)   State the type of pictorial line drawings shown above.   1

_____

(ii)   Explain why this type of view would be used.   1

_____

_____

[Turn over

MARKS | DO NOT WRITE IN THIS MARGIN

4.   (continued)

The CAD technician produced a site plan as part of the construction project and wishes to calculate the position of the lodge in relation to the plot boundary. The front of the lodge faces onto Birch Crescent.

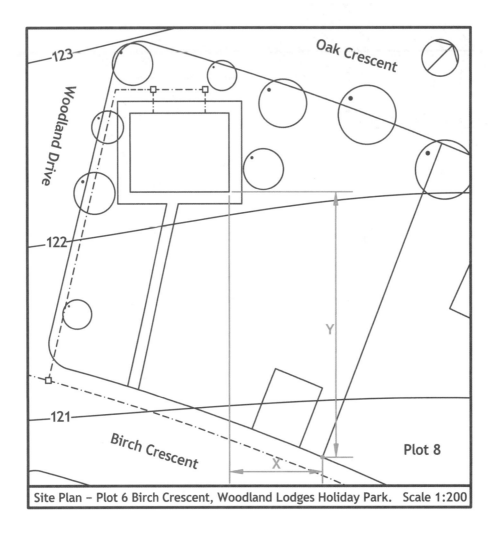

Site Plan – Plot 6 Birch Crescent, Woodland Lodges Holiday Park.   Scale 1:200

(f)   Calculate, using the scale shown, the following distances.

(i)   Distance X _____ Metres   1

(ii)   Distance Y _____ Metres   1

(g)   Identify the features drawn in red on the site plan.   1

_____

(h)   State the direction that the front of the lodge faces.   1

_____

MARKS | DO NOT WRITE IN THIS MARGIN

4. (continued)

The CAD technician produced a floor plan and enlarged detail of the lodge.

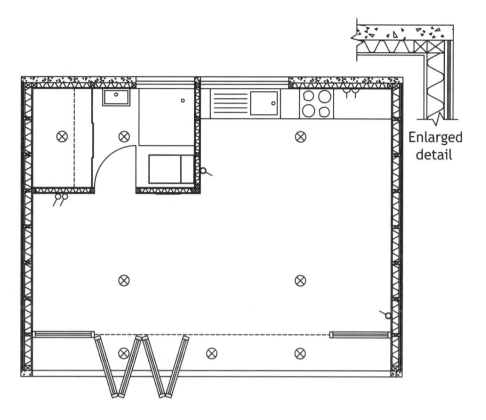

Enlarged detail

(i) Name the building drawing symbols shown below.   4

[Turn over

4. (continued)

In addition to its standard lodge, the company offers a premium range of lodges. These use modular components that allow the owners to create their own unique layout.

Elevations for three different lodge designs, A, B, and C are shown below.

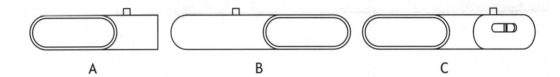

A   B   C

(j) Identify the correct pictorial view for each of the elevations above by marking **A**, **B** or **C** in the appropriate box below. You should select only one pictorial for each of the elevations.

There is only one correct answer for each elevation.

3

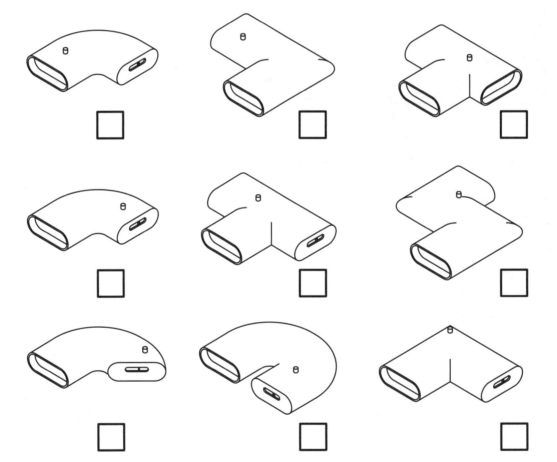

MARKS | DO NOT WRITE IN THIS MARGIN

5. A new type of bird box is produced by an environmentally conscious retailer. The lid and body are made from sheet metal. A CAD technician produced the rendered 3D CAD illustration and the pictorial line drawing shown below.

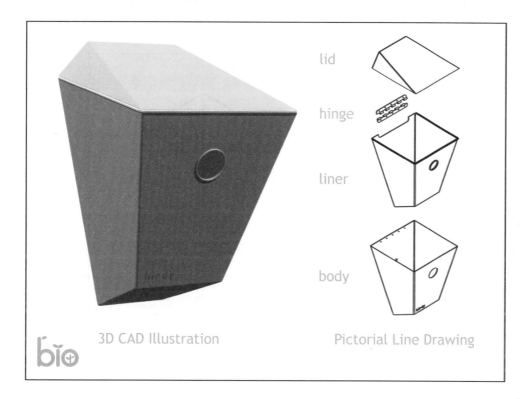

3D CAD Illustration

Pictorial Line Drawing

lid

hinge

liner

body

(a) State two reasons why the CAD technician would have produced the rendered 3D CAD illustration shown above.   **2**

_____

_____

_____

(b) State the type of pictorial line drawing shown above.   **1**

_____

(c) Describe one advantage that the pictorial line drawing has over the 3D CAD illustration.   **1**

_____

_____

[Turn over

MARKS | DO NOT WRITE IN THIS MARGIN

5. **(continued)**

The CAD technician initially created the 3D CAD illustration of the bird box. In preparing for manufacture the CAD technician has been asked to create the orthographic views shown below.

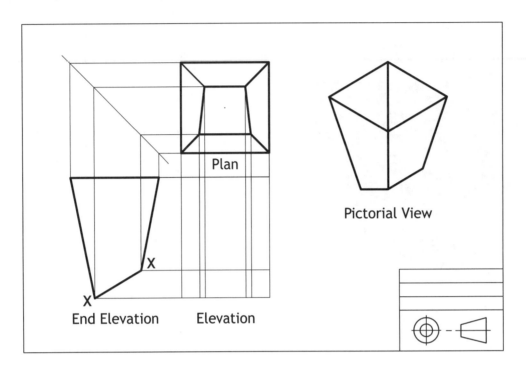

(d) Identify the correct elevation by ticking a box below. Ignore wall thickness.

1

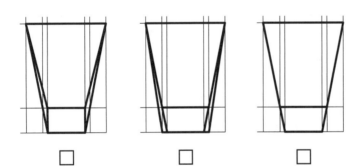

☐   ☐   ☐   ☐

(e) State two pieces of information you would find in a title block shown above other than the 3rd angle projection symbol.

2

_____

_____

MARKS | DO NOT WRITE IN THIS MARGIN

5. **(continued)**

Three line types that will be used to complete the 2D CAD drawings to British Standard conventions are shown below.

(f)   State the uses of the following line types:

   (i)   A continuous thick line.

   _____   **1**

   _____

   (ii)   A chain thin double dashed line.

   _____   **1**

   _____

   (iii)   A chain thin line.

   _____   **1**

   _____

Prior to manufacture, the CAD technician was asked to produce layouts for cutting the lid and body out of a single sheet of metal.

(g)   Explain, in terms of environmental impact, why careful consideration of the layout of multiple parts is important.   **1**

   _____

   _____

[Turn over

MARKS | DO NOT WRITE IN THIS MARGIN

5.   (continued)

A graphic designer was asked to create a 'point of sale' graphic that will be used in retail outlets to promote the bird box. The graphic designer was asked to communicate the environmental qualities of the brand. The finished graphic is shown below.

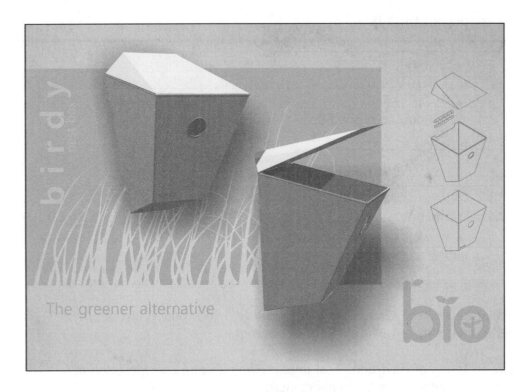

(h) Describe two ways that the designer has graphically communicated the environmental qualities of the brand.   2

_____

_____

_____

_____

_____

_____

[END OF SPECIMEN QUESTION PAPER]

MARKS | DO NOT WRITE IN THIS MARGIN

ADDITIONAL SPACE FOR ANSWERS

MARKS | DO NOT WRITE IN THIS MARGIN

ADDITIONAL SPACE FOR ANSWERS

National
Qualifications
SPECIMEN ONLY

S835/75/11

Graphic Communication
Supplementary Sheets

Date — Not applicable

Duration — 2 hours

Supplementary sheets for use with questions 2 and 3.

Supplementary sheet for use with question 2 (e)

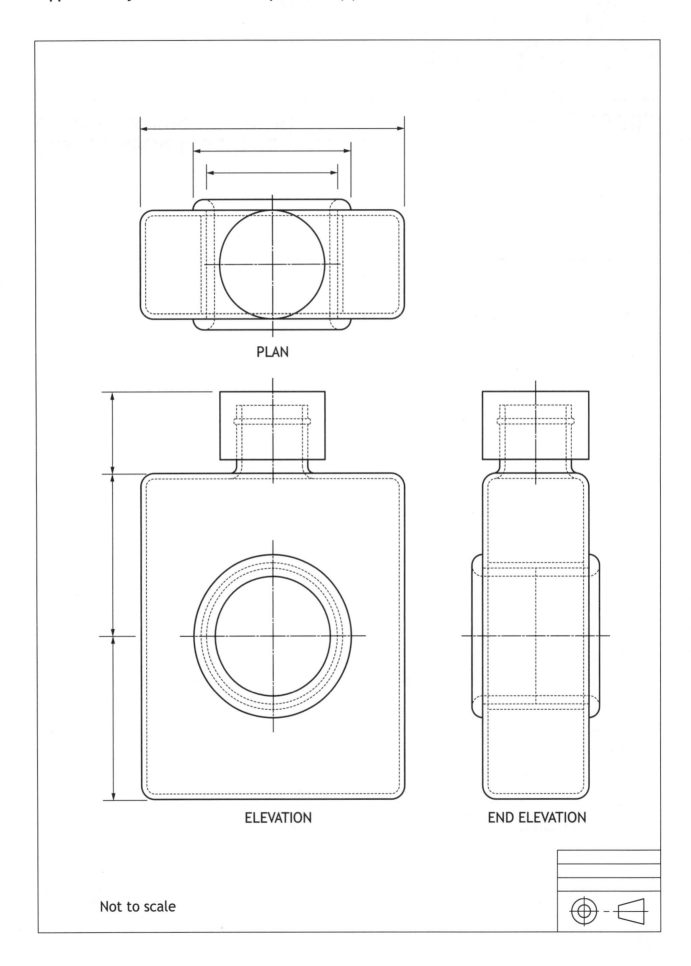

PLAN

ELEVATION

END ELEVATION

Not to scale

Supplementary sheet for use with questions 3 (a) and (b)

The orthographic drawing for the lid is shown below.

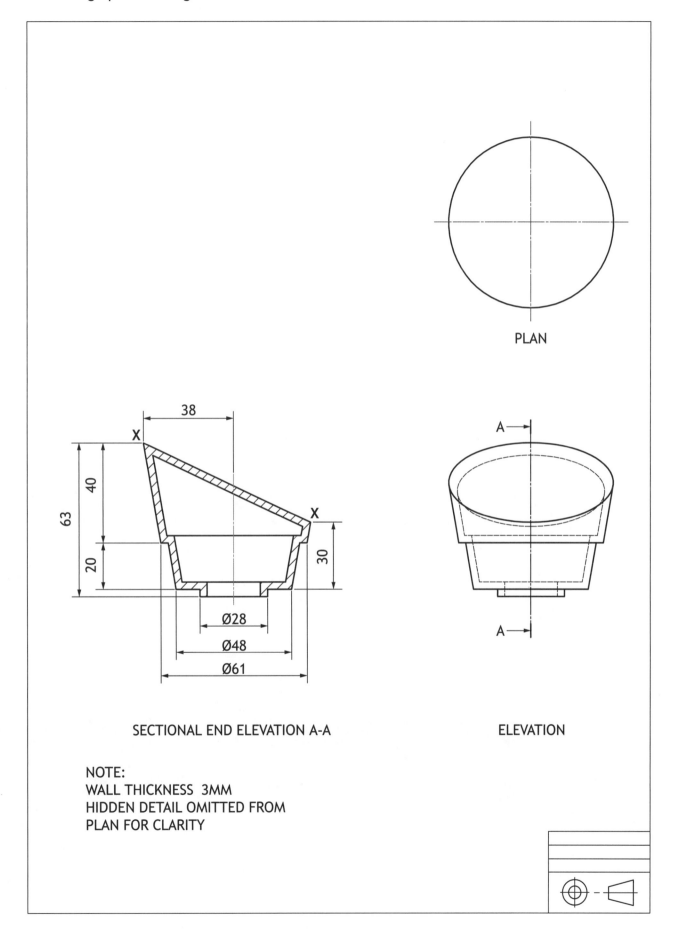

PLAN

38

X

40

63

X

20

30

Ø28

Ø48

Ø61

SECTIONAL END ELEVATION A-A

A→

A→

ELEVATION

NOTE:
WALL THICKNESS 3MM
HIDDEN DETAIL OMITTED FROM
PLAN FOR CLARITY

[BLANK PAGE]

DO NOT WRITE ON THIS PAGE

NATIONAL 5

2018

N5

National Qualifications 2018

Mark

X835/75/01

Graphic Communication

THURSDAY, 10 MAY

1:00 PM – 3:00 PM

Fill in these boxes and read what is printed below.

Full name of centre

Town

Forename(s)

Surname

Number of seat

Date of birth

Day   Month   Year   Scottish candidate number

Total marks — 80

Attempt ALL questions.

All dimensions are in mm.

All technical sketches and drawings use third angle projection.

You may use rulers, compasses or trammels for measuring.

In all questions you may use sketches and annotations to support your answer if you wish.

Write your answers clearly in the spaces provided in this booklet. Additional space for answers is provided at the end of this booklet. If you use this space you must clearly identify the question number you are attempting.

Use **blue** or **black** ink.

Before leaving the examination room you must give this booklet to the Invigilator; if you do not, you may lose all the marks for this paper.

SQA

MARKS | DO NOT WRITE IN THIS MARGIN

Total marks — 80

Attempt ALL questions

1. A knife and chopping board storage system is shown below. The body is made from sheet metal. A CAD technician produced the rendered 3D CAD illustration and the pictorial line drawing shown below.

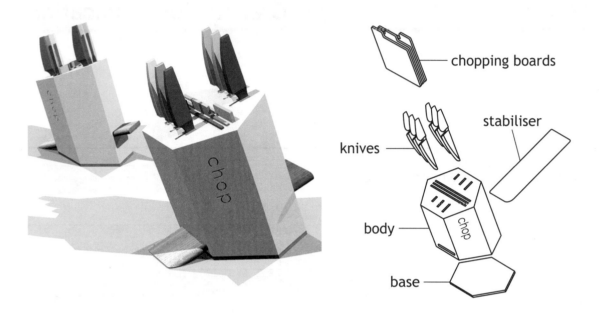

A 3D CAD model rather than a physical model of the storage system was created during the development stage.

(a) State two reasons why a 3D CAD model was more suitable than a physical model.   2

_____

_____

_____

_____

To produce the CAD model the CAD technician was given information about the storage system. One dimension stated: A/F 300mm.

(b) State the meaning of A/F.   1

_____

MARKS | DO NOT WRITE IN THIS MARGIN

1. (continued)

The CAD technician has been asked to produce an appropriate surface development for the storage system and identify where key features will be placed.

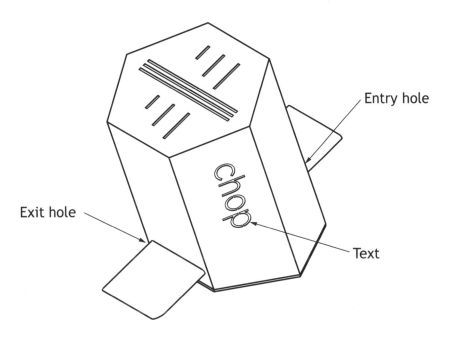

Entry hole

Exit hole

Text

(c) Indicate, on the graphic below, where the Text, Entry hole and Exit hole would be located.

Use **A** to indicate on the panel where the Text would be located.

Use **B** to indicate on the panel where the Entry hole would be located.

Use **C** to indicate on the panel where the Exit hole would be located.

3

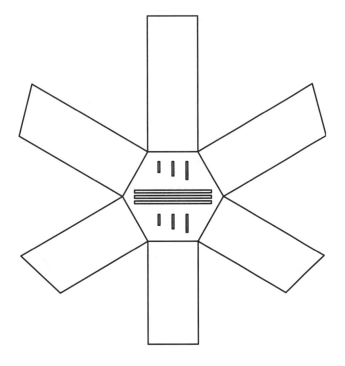

MARKS | DO NOT WRITE IN THIS MARGIN

1. (continued)

To aid the production of the storage system the CAD technician was asked to complete the orthographic drawing shown below.

Hidden detail and slots removed for clarity.

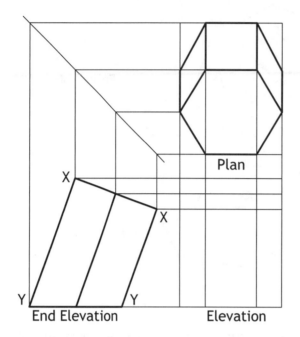

(d) Identify, using a tick (✓), the correct elevation. Ignore wall thickness.   1

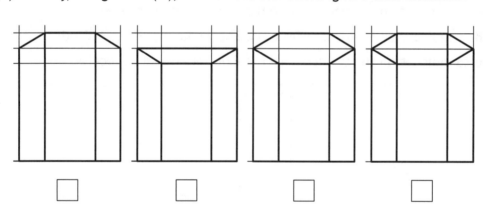

A true shape of surface X—X was required.

(e) Identify, using a tick (✓), the correct true shape. Use a ruler or trammel to measure.   1

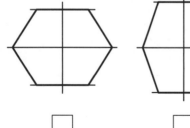
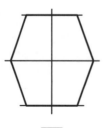
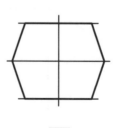
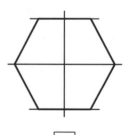

MARKS | DO NOT WRITE IN THIS MARGIN

1. **(continued)**

A true shape of surface **Y—Y** was required.

(f) Identify, using a tick (✓), the correct true shape. Use a ruler or trammel to measure.   1

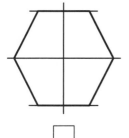   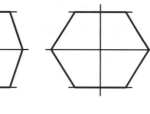

☐   ☐   ☐   ☐

[Turn over

MARKS | DO NOT WRITE IN THIS MARGIN

1. **(continued)**

The CAD technician was then asked to provide surface developments of the body of the knife block, without the top.

(g) Identify the two correct surface developments, shown opposite, of the knife block when opened out at surface generators 'A' and 'B'.

You should refer to the orthographic drawing below.

    (i) When opened out at generator A, the correct surface development is view.   1

        Insert number

    (ii) When opened out at generator B, the correct surface development is view.   1

        Insert number

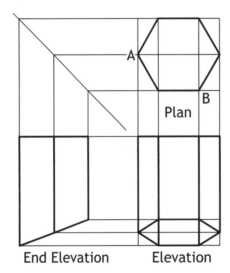

End Elevation   Elevation

MARKS | DO NOT WRITE IN THIS MARGIN

1. (continued)

The range of surface developments are show below.

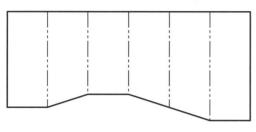

1.   2.

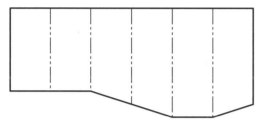

3.   4.

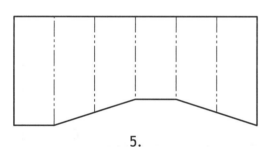

5.   6.

A number of the knife blocks are to be produced from a single sheet of material.

(h) Explain, in terms of environmental impact, why it is important to carefully consider the layout of multiple parts.   1

_____

_____

[Turn over

MARKS | DO NOT WRITE IN THIS MARGIN

1. **(continued)**

(i) A knife set to complement the knife block is to be produced. Rendered pictorials and orthographic views of one knife are shown below.

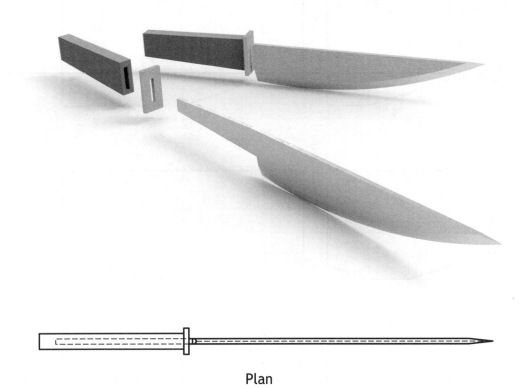

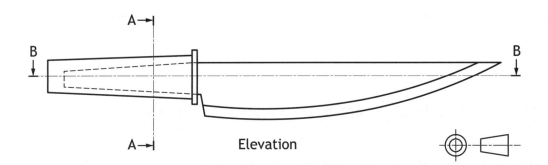

Plan

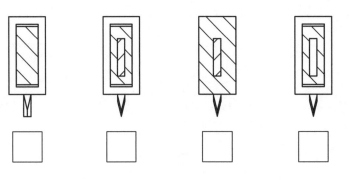

Elevation

(i) Identify the correct sectional end elevation **A-A** by ticking (✓) a box below.

1

MARKS | DO NOT WRITE IN THIS MARGIN

1. (i) (continued)

(ii) Identify the correct sectional plan **B-B** by ticking (✓) a box below.   **1**

MARKS | DO NOT WRITE IN THIS MARGIN

2. A recipe app has been produced. The graphic artist was asked to ensure that the graphic layout was easy to follow.

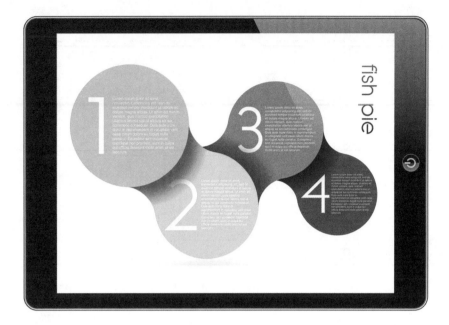

(a) Describe three ways, other than the numbering system, that the graphic artist has graphically communicated the **sequence** of the recipe shown above.

3

_____

_____

_____

_____

_____

_____

(b) Describe two benefits that producing a recipe app, rather than physically printing a recipe book, would have for the environment.

2

_____

_____

_____

_____

MARKS | DO NOT WRITE IN THIS MARGIN

2. **(continued)**

The app also contains an additional feature that analyses individual ingredients and calculates the overall health rating of the recipe.

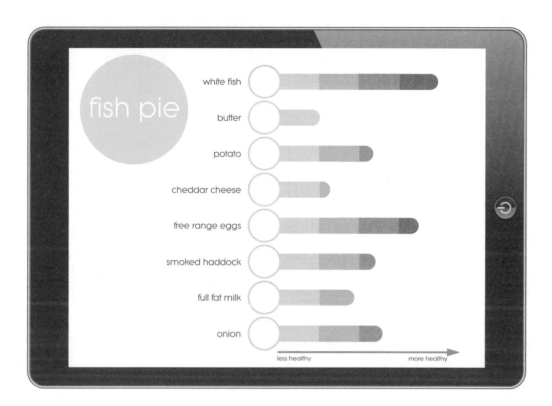

(c) Name the type of graph or chart that was used in the graphic shown above.

1

_____

(d) Describe one way that the graphic artist has graphically communicated the health rating of the individual ingredients.

1

_____

_____

[Turn over

MARKS | DO NOT WRITE IN THIS MARGIN

2.   (continued)

Two different sets of statistics that have been provided are shown below.

Statistics A	
Nutritional Data – Nuts	
Cashew	170 Calories, 13g Fat, 8g Carb, 5g Protein, 1g Fibre
Hazelnut	180 Calories, 18g Fat, 4g Carb, 4g Protein, 2g Fibre
Peanut	170 Calories, 14g Fat, 6g Carb, 7g Protein, 2g Fibre
Walnut	210 Calories, 20g Fat, 6g Carb, 5g Protein, 2g Fibre

Statistics B	
Healthy diet plan	
Fruit and Vegetables	33%
Carbohydrates	33%
Protein	12%
Milk and Dairy	15%
Fats and sugars	7%

(e)   (i)   State the most suitable type of informational graphic to present the data shown in **Statistics A**.   1

_____

(ii)   Explain why this is an appropriate type of informational graphic to present.   1

_____

_____

(f)   (i)   State the most suitable type of informational graphic to present the data in **Statistics B**.   1

_____

(ii)   Explain why this is an appropriate type of informational graphic to present.   1

_____

_____

[Turn over for next question

DO NOT WRITE ON THIS PAGE

3. A modular lighting system is shown below. There are three sizes of coloured lighting pods that can be arranged in a variety of ways. A rendered 3D CAD illustration is shown below.

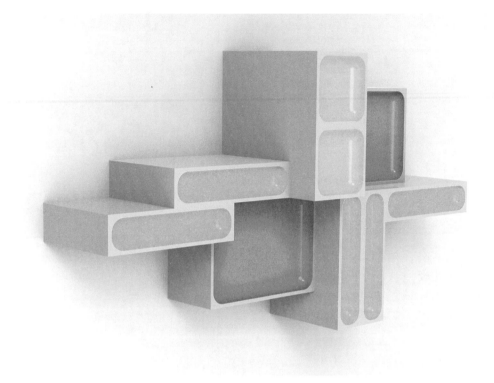

An orthographic drawing of one of the orange lighting pods is shown below.

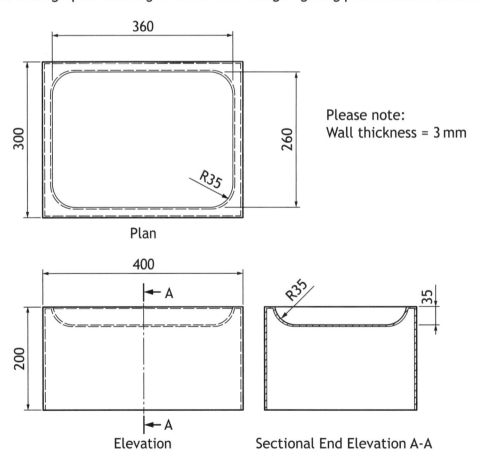

Please note:
Wall thickness = 3 mm

Plan

Elevation

Sectional End Elevation A-A

MARKS | DO NOT WRITE IN THIS MARGIN

3.　(continued)

(a)　Describe, using the correct dimensions and 3D CAD modelling terms, how you would use 3D CAD software to model the orange lighting pod. You may use sketches to support your answer.

6

3.   (continued)

Orthographic assembly views of an arrangement of the lighting system are shown below. Hidden detail removed for clarity.

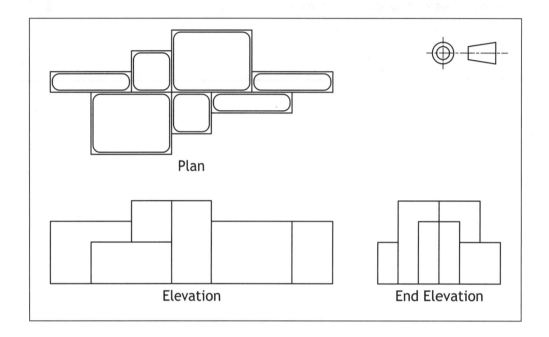

MARKS | DO NOT WRITE IN THIS MARGIN

3.   (continued)

(b)   Identify, using a tick (✓), the two pictorial assembly drawings that match
the arrangement **in the orthographic assembly drawing shown.**   2

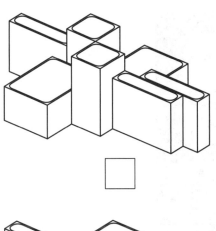

☐

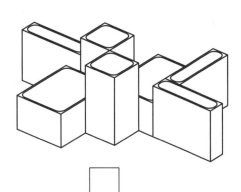

☐

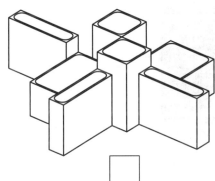

☐

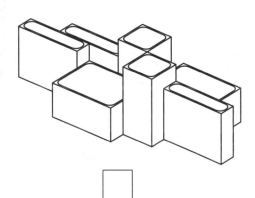

☐

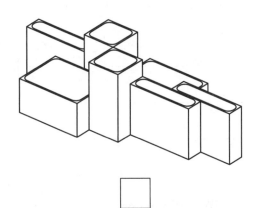

☐

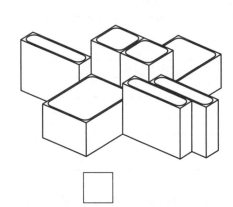

☐

[Turn over

MARKS | DO NOT WRITE IN THIS MARGIN

3.   **(continued)**

A 2D CAD line drawing, produced using 2D CAD software, and a 3D CAD model of a control panel for the lighting system are shown below.

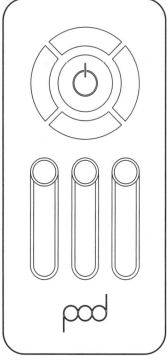

2D CAD Line Drawing

3D CAD Model

(c)   Explain why the 2D CAD line drawing can be produced more quickly than the 3D CAD model of the control panel.

1

_____

_____

_____

_____

(d)   Describe two benefits of a 3D CAD model over a 2D CAD drawing.

2

_____

_____

_____

_____

MARKS | DO NOT WRITE IN THIS MARGIN

3. (continued)

To create the features of the control panel a number of 2D CAD tools were used.

(e) State the name of the **single** CAD tool used in **each case**.   6

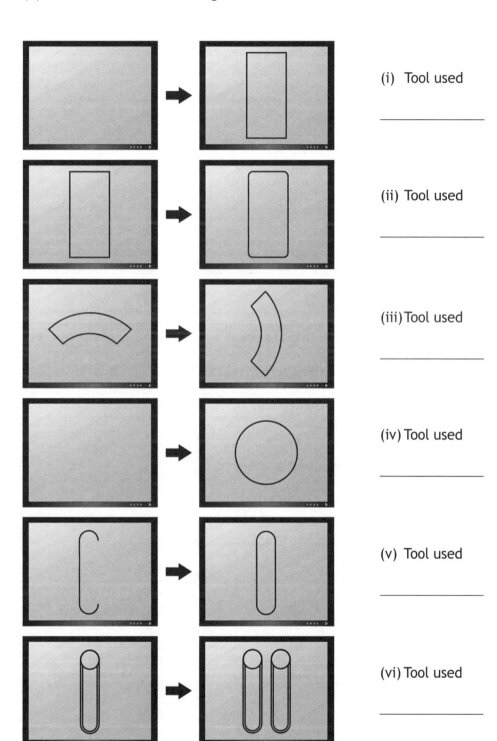

(i)   Tool used

_____

(ii) Tool used

_____

(iii) Tool used

_____

(iv) Tool used

_____

(v) Tool used

_____

(vi) Tool used

_____

MARKS | DO NOT WRITE IN THIS MARGIN

3. **(continued)**

Three line types that will be used to complete the 2D CAD drawings to British Standard conventions are shown below.

(f) State the uses of the following line types.

(i) A chain thin line   1

_ _ _ _ _ _ _ _ _

(ii) A continuous thick line   1

_____

(iii) A long dash dotted thin line, thick at ends.   1

_ _ _ _ _ _ _ _ _

The 2D CAD drawings are to be drawn using a scale.

(g) Explain what is meant by the term scale 2:1.   1

[Turn over for next question

DO NOT WRITE ON THIS PAGE

MARKS | DO NOT WRITE IN THIS MARGIN

4. A speaker has been designed using 3D CAD software. A rendered illustration is shown below.

A pictorial view of one of the speaker components is shown below.

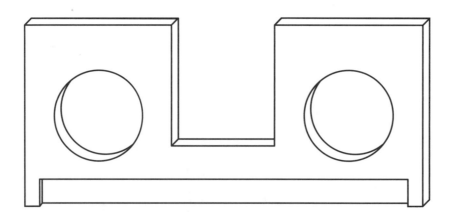

(a) State the type of pictorial view shown above.　　1

_____

MARKS | DO NOT WRITE IN THIS MARGIN

4. (continued)

A working drawing of the speaker assembly is shown below.

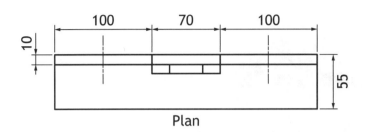

Plan

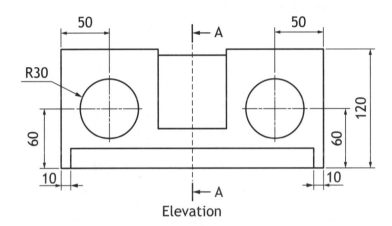

Elevation

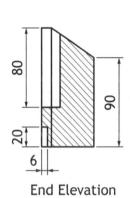

End Elevation

Five pieces of information in the working drawing do not adhere to British Standard conventions.

(b) State the five errors found in this drawing.   5

You may annotate the orthographic drawing to support your answer.

_____

_____

_____

_____

_____

4.   (continued)

Rubber feet are to be added to the base. Orthographic views and 3D illustrations of a rubber foot are shown below.

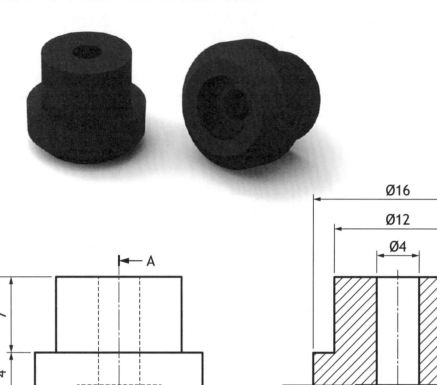

Elevation   Sectional End Elevation A-A

MARKS | DO NOT WRITE IN THIS MARGIN

4. **(continued)**

(c) Describe, using the correct dimensions and 3D CAD modelling terms, how the rubber foot, shown opposite, would be produced.

You may use sketches to support your answer.

3

MARKS | DO NOT WRITE IN THIS MARGIN

4.   **(continued)**

The orthographic drawings of the speaker were shared online.

(d) Describe two benefits of sharing these orthographic drawings online.   **2**

_____

_____

_____

_____

_____

(e) Explain why it would be useful to adhere to British Standard conventions and protocols when sharing these types of drawings.   **2**

_____

_____

_____

_____

_____

(f) Explain the purpose of the following types of production drawings.

(i) Sectional views _____   **1**

_____

_____

(ii) Assembly drawings _____   **1**

_____

_____

[Turn over for next question

DO NOT WRITE ON THIS PAGE

5. Many companies now specialise in applying promotional graphic posters, to advertise services to the public, around commercial vehicles.

A finished layout for a small building company is shown below.

MARKS | DO NOT WRITE IN THIS MARGIN

5. **(continued)**

The design work for the layout was produced by a graphic designer.

(a) Describe two ways in which the graphic designer used the following design elements and principles to enhance the layout.

(i)   Line

2

_____

_____

_____

_____

(ii) Dominance

2

_____

_____

_____

(iii) Colour

2

_____

_____

_____

(iv) Unity

2

_____

_____

_____

[Turn over

MARKS | DO NOT WRITE IN THIS MARGIN

5. **(continued)**

Vehicles were traditionally hand painted to include information about a company. Modern processes involve printing promotional graphics which are then applied to a vehicle.

Traditional painting technique

Modern printed technique

(b) Describe two advantages **to the client** of modern printing techniques over traditional painting techniques.

2

_____

_____

_____

_____

_____

_____

_____

_____

[Turn over for next question

DO NOT WRITE ON THIS PAGE

MARKS | DO NOT WRITE IN THIS MARGIN

6. A graphic designer submitted a draft layout for an architectural magazine article to the editor. The draft is shown below.

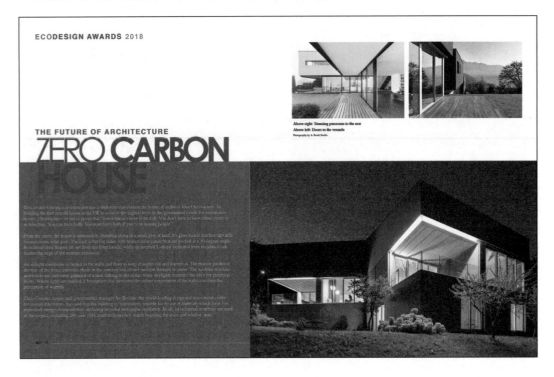

The editor provided some feedback to the graphic designer on how to improve the layout.

(a) Describe, using the feedback shown below, four improvements the graphic designer should make to the layout using **Desktop Publishing techniques**.

   (i) *The word 'house' in the heading is difficult to see*   1

   _____

   _____

   (ii) *The large column of extended text makes it difficult to read*   1

   _____

   _____

   (iii) *The bottom image would look better without the sky in the background*   1

   _____

   _____

   (iv) *The body text is too close to the edge of the paper*   1

   _____

   _____

MARKS | DO NOT WRITE IN THIS MARGIN

6.　(continued)

The graphic designer used a sans serif font for the heading.

(b)　State two reasons why the graphic designer has chosen a sans serif font for the heading.　　**2**

_____

_____

_____

_____

_____

When inserting an image, the graphic designer used the handles of the image to increase its size. This resulted in the image being out of proportion, shown below.

(c)　Describe how the graphic designer could have resized the image without altering the proportions.　　**1**

_____

_____

_____

MARKS | DO NOT WRITE IN THIS MARGIN

6.   **(continued)**

During the production of the layout, using desktop publishing software, the graphic designer used **guidelines**.

(d)   Describe two advantages of using guidelines in the creation of promotional layouts.

2

_____

_____

_____

_____

[END OF QUESTION PAPER]

Candidates please note that in the official exam there are two Additional Space for Answer pages that are not included in this version for reasons of space.

NATIONAL 5

Answers

NATIONAL 5 GRAPHIC COMMUNICATION 2017

1. (a) (i) • Clear view of each component of the product
    • Shows assembly order/fit together
    • Easier to understand by a wider audience (non-technical person)

  (ii) • All component parts are in view
    • All component parts are correctly aligned
    • There is day-light (clearance) between all component parts
    • All component parts are assembled in sequence
    • Uniform distance of exploded parts

(b)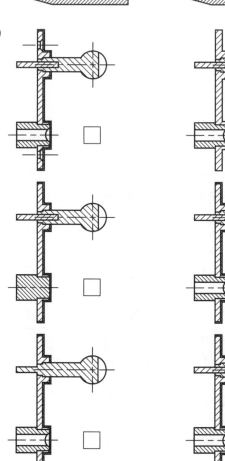

(c)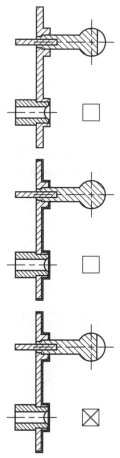

(d)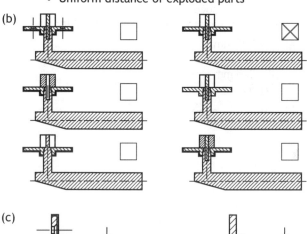

(e) • Hatching runs in opposite direction
    • Vary the spacing/pitch of hatching
    • Vary the angle of hatching (other than 45°)

(f) Any two from:
    • Webs
    • Axle/shaft
    • Screws
    • Bolts
    • Nuts
    • Pins
    • Holes
    • Voids
    • Washer

(g) Revolve approach:
    • Create initial profile making reference to correct dimensions   1
    • Revolve 360 degrees around centre axis   1
    • Create triangle profile/sketch making reference to correct dimensions   1
    • Subtract required material   1

2. (a) (i) Alignment
    • Logo left aligned with body text
    • 'Blic' brand left aligned with orange strap line/Sub-heading
    • Body text aligned with top of 'blic' brand
    • Coloured logos aligned centrally/horizontal
    • Bottom of letter 'C' on brand aligned with 'arm' of seating plan view
    • Bottom of seating plan view aligned with bottom of logos

  (ii) Unity
    • Unity created through alignment
    • Unity created through colour
    • Text and graphic make use of outline
    • Background image ties many of the elements together

  (iii) Contrast
    • Reference to any two contrasting colours on the layout
    • Outlined and rendered graphics
    • Reference to the contrast between dark graphic and 'blic' outlined text
    • Size of text

(b) • Information conveyed quickly
    • Exposure to audience is time limited
    • Eye catching design to create instant interest
    • Information is kept to a minimum
    • Large dominant image

(c) • Ensures correct alignment
    • Effective spacing
    • Allows a good level of accuracy
    • Speeds up process
    • Negates use of guides
    • Assist in sizing of objects

(d)

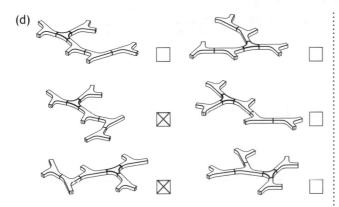

☐   ☐

⊠   ☐

⊠   ☐

(e) (i) Mirror
 (ii) • Guarantees level of accuracy/symmetry
  • Time saved by not having to redraw

(f) (i) Subtraction
 (ii) Fillet
 (iii) Chamfer

(g) (i)

Constraint used Align

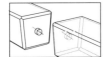
Constraint used Centre Axis

Constraint used Mate

OR

Constraint used Align

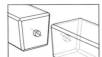
Constraint used Centre Axis

Constraint used Mate

OR

Constraint used Align

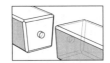
Constraint used Align

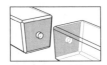
Constraint used Mate

OR

Constraint used Align

Constraint used Align

Constraint used Mate

 (ii) • Same component can be used over and over
  • No need to re-draw repeated components
  • Less chance of errors
  • Speeds up production
  • Standardisation

3. (a)

Bottom Tile	Top Tile	Resultant Colour
Red	Yellow	**ORANGE**
Yellow	**BLUE**	Green
Blue	**RED**	Violet

(b) • Black/grey is added to create a shade

(c) • Allows different elements of the app to stand out and be easily recognisable by the user
 • Eye catching
 • Creates visual interest/excitement
 • Appeal to target audience

(d) (i) Fold Line
 (ii) Centre Line

4. (a) Pie chart

(b) • Illustrates and compares percentages
 • Each segment is proportional to the quantity it represents

 • A segment has a dedicated colour to differentiate it from other segments

(c) • Colour picking process (accept any response that clearly describes the process of colour picking and the tools involved)
 • Note the colour codes of a graphic (Pantone, CMYK or RGB acceptable) and apply consistently to other graphics
 • Copy and paste a graphic **and manipulate**
 • Make use of a standard colour palette

(d) • Use recycled materials for the cards and packaging
 • Cards and packaging can be made from recyclable materials
 • Print the cards using soy inks/sustainable inks
 • Use less ink
 • Ensure no spacing between cards to reduce amount of waste card
 • Smaller card size
 • Reduce gauge of card
 • Reduce the amount of material used for packaging

5. (a) (i) 200 mm
 (ii) 160 mm
 (iii) 280 mm
 (iv) 50 mm

(b) (i)

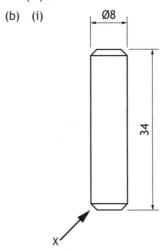

 (ii) Chamfer

(c)

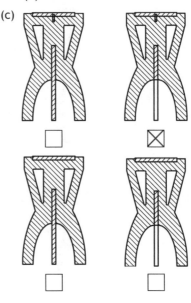

☐   ⊠

☐   ☐

(d)

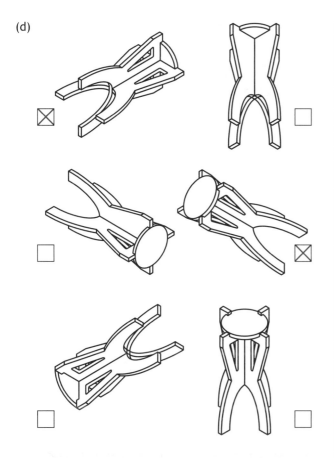

NATIONAL 5 GRAPHIC COMMUNICATION 2017 SPECIMEN QUESTION PAPER

1. (a) Any two from:
- Generate ideas quickly
- Generate a range of ideas
- Allow for evaluation of ideas
- Ideas can be shared with the client

(b) Any three from:
- Layer function can be used to overlap elements
- Ease of editing
- Images can be manipulated
- Variety of fonts are available to try
- Grid/guide tools can be used to enable accurate alignment of elements
- Speed of production
- Layouts and files can be sent long distances via email, remote working share with client
- Wide range of colour schemes available
- Access to a wide range of media
- Layout would be more accurate

Or any other relevant advantage that is related to the context

(c) Any two from:
- Creates unity
- Green colour has a calming effect
- Harmonises with the blue
- Sound wave line relates to the product
- Contrasting wave against horizontal lines creates visual impact
- Depth created by wave line
- Depth created by gaps in straight lines
- Use of line leads the eye across whole page

(d) (i) Depth:
Any two from:
- Overlapping of various elements
- Faded background image appears further away
- Drop shadow on the pictorial gives illusion of depth

(ii) Dominance:
Any two from:
- Focal point is created by large exploded view
- Bold and capitalised text
- Faded image recedes and makes the exploded view more dominant *(2 marks for identification and justification)*
- Smaller images are scaled down to make the focal point more dominant *(2 marks for identification and justification)*

(iii) Alignment:
Any two from:
- Vertical alignment of heading with other written content makes the layout feel organised and structured *(2 marks for identification and justification)*
- Horizontal/central alignment of heading with small icons and/or horizontal green line also makes the page appear structured and organised *(2 marks for identification and justification)*
- Horizontal alignment of Bluetooth logo with green line/text
- Top of green wave aligned with bottom of speaker
- Bottom of speaker aligned with bottom of green wave
- Alignment of text elements on left hand side of page

(e) Any one from:
- Transparency has been used to make sure the background graphic does not distract from the main focus of the promotional item
- To make the speaker stand out more

(f) Any one from:
- The line/image/wave runs off the edge of the advert
- The image overlaps the side/edge of the advert/webpage

(g) Any two from:
- No ink would be used
- No paper would be used
- No surplus of posters would be wasted
- No transport required to take posters around the country/world
- Only consumers interested in the product would use a webpage

Any other relevant environmental benefit

2. (a) Any two from:
- Make packaging from recyclable/biodegradable materials
- Make packaging from recycled materials
- Reduce the amount of material used for packaging
- Environmentally friendly inks
- Limit amount of ink being used
- Reusable packaging
- Highlight recyclability of materials
- Efficient layout of multiple parts when manufacturing

(b)

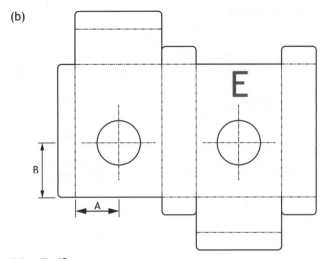

(c) (i) 40 mm
(ii) 50 mm

(d) Any one from:
- Size of media
- Size of object
- Level of detail
- Drawing type

(e) (i) Chain dimensioning
(ii) Parallel dimensioning

(f)

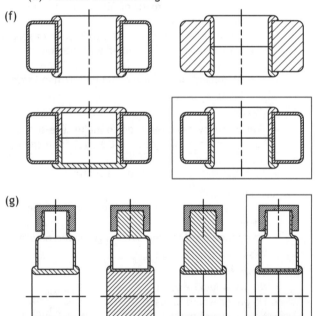

(g)

3. (a) Revolve approach:
1. Initial profile correctly dimensioned   2
2. Revolve   1
3. Dimensioned and correctly positioned angled profile   1
4. Subtraction of all appropriate material   1
5. Shell, 3 mm wall thickness and remove correct face (underside)   1

Extrusion approach:
1. ⌀28 circle, extrude 3 mm   1
2. ⌀48 circle, taper extrude 20 mm   1
3. ⌀61 circle, taper extrude 40 mm   1
4. Dimensioned and correctly positioned profile   1
5. Subtraction of all appropriate material   1
6. Shell, 3 mm wall thickness and remove correct face (underside)   1

NB. Taper angle not required

Loft approach:
1. ⌀28 circle, extrude 3 mm   1
2. ⌀48 loft to ⌀55, 20 mm between profiles   1
3. ⌀61 loft to ⌀76, 40 mm between profiles   1
4. Dimensioned and correctly positioned profile   1
5. Subtraction of all appropriate material   1
6. Shell, 3 mm wall thickness and remove correct face (underside)   1

(b)

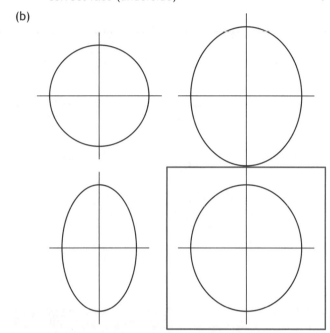

(c) Draw 2 arcs — 1 mark (must use term 'arc')   1
Vertical & horizontal lines to join up profile   1
Mirror & axis (single profile) (top)   1
Mirror & axis (two profiles) (bottom)   1

(d) Modelling Tree edit that moves shell command after the extrude command in the modelling tree   2

(e) Centre axis   1
Shading of appropriate surface   1

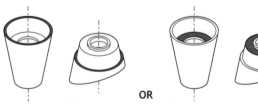

                                            OR

Mate   1

4. (a) (i) Promotional
(ii) Any one from:
- Used to promote the product, company, service
- Provide potential customers with an idea of what the finished construction project will look like
- They can appear 'less technical' than production drawings
- They tend to be more easily understood then production drawings

(b) (i) Reverse
(ii) Transparency
(iii) Sub-heading
(iv) Body text/column
(v) Footer

(c) Any two from:
- Easy to send electronically to relevant people
- Easy to collaborate with more people in different locations
- Allows 24 hour working globally
- Option to work at different locations other than their own office
- Reduction in need to travel

(d) (i) Location plan
    (ii) 1:1250

(e) (i) Oblique OR cabinet oblique
    (ii) Any one from
    - It is the preferred option when there are circles or radii involved in the front view — as is the case with the lodge
    - Ability to show an accurate elevation but also giving the impression of 3D form

(f) (i) *X = 5 Metres*
    (ii) *Y = 14 Metres*

(g) Contour lines

(h) South East

(i) Sinktop   Switch
    Wash basin   Lamp

(j)

A   B

C

5. (a) Any two from:
- The graphic can be used for promotional/marketing reasons
- The graphic can aid discussions with the client prior to manufacture
- This type of graphic is more universally understood
- This type of graphic is more easily understood by non-technical people
- Provides a realistic representation of the product

(b) Exploded isometric view.

(c) Any one from:
- This type of graphic is more **informative** than the 3D CAD illustration
- It lets the viewer see how the product is assembled
- It lets the viewer see all the component parts of the product

(d)
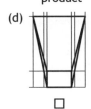   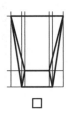
☐ ☐ ☒ ☐

(e) Any two from:
- Project title
- Name of draughtsperson
- Start date/completion date or print date
- Scale
- Drawing number/sheet number
- Dimensional tolerances
- Dimensional units used
- Document/drawing type

(f) (i) Visible outlines and edges
    (ii) Bend lines/fold lines
    (iii) Centre lines

(g) Any answer which details a reduction of waste materials or environmental concerns

(h) Any two from:
- Use of natural textures such as the grass
- Green colour scheme is instantly recognisable with eco products
- Colour green is recognisable as being linked to nature, outdoors and similar connotations
- Brown 'natural' background/printed on brown 'natural' paper
- Printed on brown paper
- Logo directly references nature/natural environment
- Amount of ink used has been kept to a minimum (lots of white space/line drawing uses less)

NATIONAL 5 GRAPHIC COMMUNICATION 2018

1. (a) Any two from:
- Easier to modify
- Can be used for illustrative purposes
- Can be easily used for testing and/or simulation
- Speed of production
- Can be electronically shared
- Saves on materials

(b) Across Flats only

(c)
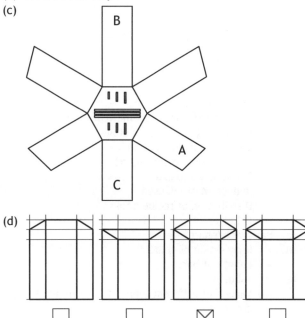

(d)
☐ ☐ ☒ ☐

(e)

(f)

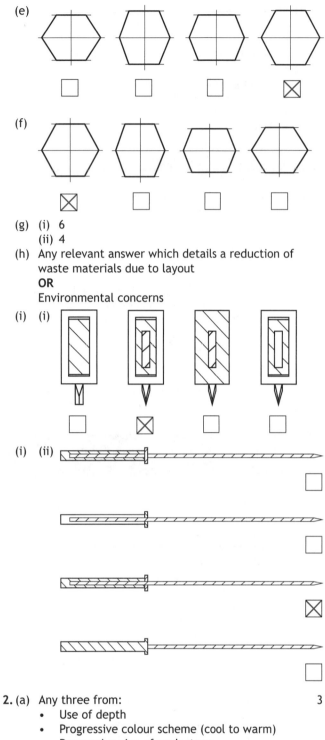

(g) (i) 6
(ii) 4

(h) Any relevant answer which details a reduction of waste materials due to layout
OR
Environmental concerns

(i) (i)

(i) (ii)

2. (a) Any three from: 3
- Use of depth
- Progressive colour scheme (cool to warm)
- Decreasing size of each stage
- Left to right progression
- All sections are connected

(b) • Reduction of paper
- Reduction of ink used
- Distribution of recipe books
- Pollution

(c) Bar graph/chart

(d) • Progression of colours
- Length of bars

(e) (i) Table
(ii) Variety of different types of information to be conveyed

(f) (i) Pie Chart
(ii) • Shows percentages
- Proportions of a whole

3. (a) One mark for each of the following:
- Initial profile 300x400mm
- Extrude 200mm
- Sketch on top surface 360x260mm
- Subtract 35mm
- Fillet all (8) edges of the subtracted section r35
- Shell 3mm removing bottom surface

(b)

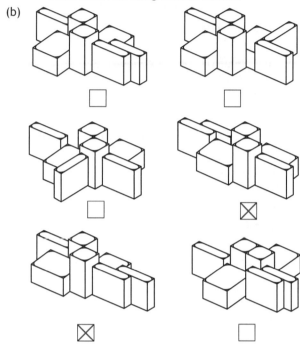

(c) Any one from:
- No depth to produce
- No multiple components to assemble
- Fewer steps required

(d) Any two from:
- Model can be manipulated to be viewed 360 degrees
- More realistic
- Depth is visible
- Imported into an environment
- Lighting effects can be applied to 3D models
- Can enable CAD/CAM
- Simulation and animation

(e) (i) Rectangle
(ii) Fillet
(iii) Rotate
(iv) Circle
(v) Line
(vi) Copy

(f) (i) Centre lines
(ii) Visible edges and outlines
(iii) Cutting plane

(g) Drawing would be twice real-world size

4. (a) Oblique
(b) Response should include:
- Plan wrong orientation
- Cutting plane
- Radius of circle
- Hatching running same direction on neighbouring parts
- Depth of 55mm on wrong side of dimension line
- Label on 'sectional end elevation'
- Centre line missing on end elevation
- Inconsistent arrowheads

(c) **Revolve with hole approach**
- 2D sketch of profile with correct dimensions   1
- Correct offset and identification of Centre axis   1
- Revolve 360 degrees   1

Revolve without hole approach
- 2D sketch of profile with correct dimensions   1
- Revolve 360 degrees (axis must be obvious)   1
- Removal of hole   1
  - Profile Ø8
  - Subtract 3mm
  - Profile Ø4
  - Subtract all

Extrusion approach
- Profile Ø16   **1 mark for 4 stages**
- Extrude 6mm
- Profile Ø12
- Extrude 7mm

- Chamfer 2mm   **1 mark for chamfer**

- Profile Ø8   **1 mark for 4 stages**
- Subtract 3mm
- Profile Ø4
- Subtract all

(d) Response should cover the topic areas below:
- Shipping impact
- Pollution
- Printing materials
- Immediacy of access
- Reaching wider audience
- Allows easy access for others to modify
- Open source format allows others to manufacture it

(e) Any two from:
- Common language
- Aids comprehension
- Multiple people working on same project

(f) (i) Any one from:
- To show internal details
- Distinguishes how different parts of a product fit together

(ii) Any one from:
- Indicate how a product with multiple parts goes together
- Show the product with all components in the correct position

5. (a) (i) Any two from:
- Layering of lines to create depth
- Lines run parallel with website drawing attention
- Physical connection between title and large logo
- Leads eye across the page

(ii) Any two from:
- Contrasting colours
- Large/bold title dominates page
- Quartered circles dominate due to scale
- Use of partially transparent box to fade out background and make title more dominant

(iii) Any two from:
- Harmonising colours in background
- Contrasting brand and website
- Receding colours in background

(iv) Any two from:
- Colour
- Line
- Shape
- Typeface
- Alignment
- Positioning of elements
The response must refer to the relationship between separate items

(b) Any two from:
- More complex images can be produced
- Larger range of colours
- Easy to replace/renew
- Faster application process
- Accuracy of print
- Repeatability

6. (a) (i) Any one from:
- Use reverse text
- Change colour to make more visible

(ii) Any one from:
- Increase number of columns
- Use column rule
- Introduction of a gutter

(iii) Crop image

(iv) Any one from:
- Increase the size of left hand margin
- Resize text box

(b) Any two from:
- Clean looking
- Modern
- Easy to read
- Sans serif font reflects the style of the building

(c) Any one from:
- Use corners/corner handles (use of shift and/or ctrl accepted)
- Scale

(d) Any two from:
- Aids alignment
- Aids accuracy
- Aids structure
- Description of being moveable
- Visibility can be turned on/off
- Elements can be snapped to them
- Can be bespoke to individual layouts or multiple layouts (master pages)

Acknowledgements

Permission has been sought from all relevant copyright holders and Hodder Gibson is grateful for the use of the following:

Image © Suradech Prapairat/Shutterstock.com (2017 page 19);
The Bluetooth® word mark and logos are registered trademarks owned by the Bluetooth SIG, Inc. and any use of such marks by Hodder Gibson is under license (2017 SQP page 4);
Image © S. Blackwell Signs & Painting (2018 page 30);
Image © Popular Mechanics (Hearst Communications, Inc.) (2018 page 30);
Image © alexandre zveiger/stock.adobe.com (2018 page 32);
Image © Pozzoli Luigi via alexandre zveiger/stock.adobe.com (2018 page 32);
Image © alexandre zveiger/stock.adobe.com (2018 pages 32 & 33).